MIDLAND RED
DOUBLE-DECKERS

DAVID HARVEY

AMBERLEY

Front cover above: 2249, (FHA 231), has just arrived in Kidderminster at the Bull Ring from Birmingham on the 133 service. It is about to depart for Stourport, which had been built alongside the River Severn in the late eighteenth century as England's only purpose-built canal new town. 2249 entered service in February 1939 and, about ten years later, was due for its rebuild by Hooton in 1950. In this, its original body condition, the subtle curves of the un-rebuilt Brush bodywork really enhances the appearance of the bus. (J. Fozard)

Front cover below: Parked in St Margaret's Bus Station, Leicester, with Burleys Way in the background, 4976, (2976 HA), a BMMO D9 with a Carlyle H40/32R bodywork, entered service in April 1962 from Wigston Garage, where it remained until withdrawn in April 1974. Unlike most BMMO D9s, this bus went to Thomas Morris & Son of Pencoed for nearly another two years' service. The destination display suggests that the bus just might be going back to South Wigston on the L8 route! (D. F. Parker)

Rear cover: The B87 route was operated by Midland Red as the longest of eight routes on the Dudley Road corridor, which had replaced the former Birmingham & Midland Tramways Co. tram services on 1 October 1939. Midland Red operated the B84–B87 services, which ran beyond Smethwick. 4372, (VHA 372), a BMMO D7 with a Metro-Cammell H32/26R bodywork that was allocated to Oldbury Garage for the whole of its life, negotiates the Oldbury Road traffic island at the junction with Rood End Road when operating on the B87 service, which had a 10-minute headway. (A. D. Broughall)

First published 2017

Amberley Publishing
The Hill, Stroud
Gloucestershire, GL5 4EP

www.amberley-books.com

British Library Cataloguing in Publication Data.
A catalogue record for this book is available from the British Library.

ISBN 978 1 4456 6786 7 (print)
ISBN 978 1 4456 6787 4 (ebook)

Typeset in 10pt on 13pt Sabon.
Typesetting and Origination by Amberley Publishing.
Printed in the UK.

Contents

Acknowledgements

The author is grateful to the many photographers acknowledged in the text who have contributed to this volume. I sincerely thank all of those who are still alive for allowing me to use pictures, many of which were taken more than sixty years ago. Thanks are also due to the late Roy Marshall, Les Mason and Peter Yeomans, who all printed photographs for me many years ago and generously gave permission for me to use their material. Where the photographer is not known, the photographs are credited to my own collection. Special thanks are due to my wife Diana for her splendid proof reading.

The book would not have been possible without the continued encouragement given by Connor Stait at Amberley Publishing.

1902–1911: The Pioneering Early Years

On 1 January 1902, the British Electric Traction group acquired the City of Birmingham Tramways Co. Since the late 1870s, CBT were operating services in the city that included horse trams to Nechells, cable trams to Handsworth, an extensive network of steam tram services to Kings Heath, Sparkhill, Small Heath, Saltley and Perry Barr, and the first overhead electric tramcars in Birmingham to Selly Oak, which had replaced the accumulator battery trams in 1901. In addition they also were operating about 100 horse buses on the Warwick Road and Hagley Road routes, as well as the service to Harborne.

The first regular use of a motorbus was on 8 September 1902, when a Mr W. W. Greener charged 2*d* for the 1½ mile journey between Erdington Green and Salford Bridge. The Birmingham Motor Express Co., set up by the Birmingham & Midland Tramways Co., was formed to use motorbuses between Birmingham Town Hall and the Plough and Harrow Hotel on Hagley Road. Early in 1903 a Milnes-Daimler wagonette was used as a trial on this route. By October 1903 the BME were operating three vehicles. As this was before the first registration numbers were issued (after the passing of the Motor Car Act, which came into force on 1 January 1904), they can be identified by their licence plate numbers: 251 was a single-deck bus twelve-seater Mulliner while 291 and 292 were Mulliner charabancs with steeply raked 'torpedo-style' open bodywork.

In December 1903, the Birmingham & Motor Express Co. purchased six Milnes-Daimler 16-hp thirty-six-seat double-deck buses, registered O 264–269. By 12 April 1904 a 20-minute service between the Grammar School in New Street along Hagley Road to the Bear Hotel, Bearwood, was being operated. A further nine 24-hp Milnes-Daimlers, registered O 1270–8, entered service in January 1905 with only seats for thirty. All the Milnes-Daimlers were painted in a natural wood colour, lined in yellow and with green wheels. In March 1905, a Thornycroft 24-hp thirty-seater, O 1279, was hired from the London Motor Omnibus Co. and was used until November 1905. In February 1905, BME also purchased O 1280, a German Dürkopp 20-hp import, painted in a lake livery with yellow panels. In the same month, a pair of Birmingham-manufactured semi-forward control thirty-six-seat Wolseley 20-hp two-cylindered chassis arrived in a chocolate livery, registered O 1281 and 1282. Meanwhile the City of Birmingham Tramways introduced a competing motorbus service to Harborne that operated four further Dürkopps, registered O 1301–1304, in May 1905.

On 26 November 1904, the directors of the BME registered a new company: the Birmingham & Midland Motor Omnibus Co. Limited. On 1 June 1905 BMMO took over the horse bus and motorbus operations of the BME and those of the

City of Birmingham Tramways Co. The livery chosen was the red specified by the Birmingham General Omnibus Co. in 1900, with black mudguards. At first, the buses carried the BET magnet and wheel emblem, but soon the fleet name 'MIDLAND', in gold letters with black shading, appeared and the name 'Midland Red' was born. By 1 August 1905, the new BMMO company commenced motorbus operations in its own right. Between October 1906 and January 1907 O 1283–1291, nine new Brush B types with French-built 40-hp Mutel engines, entered service, but with indifferent reliability. Birmingham Corporation's Municipal Watch Committee refused to allow the operation of motor omnibuses running on tramway routes and, when ten new Corporation tram routes were opened on 1 January 1907, along with the compulsory purchase of former CBT tram routes in the city, any existing omnibus services on the tram routes had to be withdrawn.

With many of the surviving motorbuses buses having increasing numbers of breakdowns, BMMO decided to replace all the motorbuses and revert to horse omnibuses from 5 October 1907 on both the Hagley Road and Harborne routes. It is worth noting that these two prestigious suburbs of western Birmingham were always resistant to any form of public road transport. Birmingham Corporation had great difficulty in getting the tram route along Hagley Road opened because of the objections of local residents, as it competed with and eventually killed off the competition from the higher status Harborne Railway. As regards gaining tramway access into Harborne, attempts had been rejected as early as the autumn of 1906 and were never revived.

The almost new Brush vehicles were in good condition and were transferred to operate in Deal, Kent, with five of them receiving new Birch Brothers charabanc bodies. The three remaining Brush buses went on hire to the Leamington & Warwick Electrical Co. in March 1908. The Five Ways premises, spares and machinery were sold at auction in September 1908, so that only the double-deck bodies from eight Milnes-Daimlers and three Dürkopps survived at West Smethwick depot at the end of 1908. In 1910, a Daimler KPL petrol-electric double-decker, registered DU 1251, with an all-metal green-liveried body, was unsuccessfully operated on the Hagley Road route for three months commencing on 1 December 1911.

O264

Opposite above: The first successful motorbuses bought by the Birmingham Motor Express Co. were six Milnes-Daimler 20-hp double-deckers with Milnes O18/16RO bodies. O 264 was the first of the batch, entering service on 12 April 1904 on a service from King Edward VI School in New Street to the Bear Hotel, Bearwood, by way of Broad Street, Five Ways, the Ivy Bush and Hagley Road. On a sunny day in 1904, this pioneering bus, well loaded, especially with adventurous young women on the open top deck, travels though Victoria Square towards Broad Street, with the Head Post Office, designed by Sir Henry Tanner and completed in 1891, in the background. (D. R. Harvey collection)

O264–268

Above: Speeding along Hagley Road, flat out at 12 mph, is one of the O264–268 batch of 16-hp Milnes Daimlers with Milnes O18/18RO bodywork that had entered service on 12 April 1904. The bus is travelling into the city and has just passed Monument Road. It is approaching the Oratory of St Philip Neri Roman Catholic Church, which is located behind the trees. Behind the original early 1860s Renaissance-styled school buildings is the current church, constructed between 1907 and 1910 in a Baroque design as a memorial to Cardinal John Newman. (Commercial Postcard)

O1274

The Holt Brewery Co. opened Ye Olde Kings Head in Hagley Road in 1905. The pub was still looking new when O1274, one of the 24-hp Milnes-Daimlers with a Milnes O18/12RO body, had arrived at the terminus, which at that time was also the City boundary. The bus had entered service with Birmingham Motor Express in October 1904 and wore a natural wood colour livery, lined in yellow. It survived until the cessation of motorbus operation on 5 October 1907. (Commercial Postcard)

O1281

In February 1905 a pair of Wolseley double-deckers with 20-hp two-cylinder engines entered service with the Birmingham Motor Express Co. These buses had a semi-forward control layout, which was quite unusual for the time, with the driver sitting above the engine. The bodies had an O18/12RO layout, though some sources state that they were thirty-six-seaters. O1281 is parked in Lordswood Road immediately after entering service. (D. R. Harvey collection)

O1283–1291

The most successful of Birmingham Motor Express's motorbuses were nine Brush 40-hp B types. They entered service in January 1907 but were all withdrawn on 5 October 1907, along with all the other motorbuses, and were sold by early 1908. It is at the Ivy Bush and is fully loaded with passengers, suggesting that they were masters of the steady climbs along the Hagley Road route. The bus is carrying an advertisement for Stephenson's Cigarettes, whose best-known brand was a Turkish blend called Sultan's Pride. (D. R. Harvey collection)

O1291

O1291 stands alongside The Talbot Hotel in Hagley Road facing the city centre, having turned round at the nearby Bear Hotel terminus. This Brush B bus, powered by a French-built Mutel 40-hp engine, had a Milnes O18/18RO body and was painted in the BET Group's green livery with the magnet transfer on the side panelling. O1291 later went on loan to the Leamington Spa District Co. to augment local tram services. (D. R. Harvey collection)

1912–1914: Getting Established

In 1912, Midland Red made another attempt to introduce motorbuses on the Hagley Road route with L. G. Wyndham Shire as the chief engineer and it was his influence that really dragged the company into the forefront of motorbus operation over the next three decades. The same 'corridor' out of the city was chosen with the new buses being employed again on the Hagley Road service to Bearwood, which had still to receive its Corporation tram service, and also to Harborne, where the new bus service terminated at the Duke of York public house.

This time petrol-electric Tilling-Stevens TTA1 double-deckers were chosen, as these petrol-electrics had a proven reliability in London and, with their lack of gears, made it easier for horse-bus drivers to learn to drive them. The chassis had 13-foot 6-inch wheelbases and a 30-hp motor, with a distinctive Renault-style 'coal-scuttle' bonnet with the radiator fitted on the bulkhead. The buses had Tilling O18/16RO bodies and were very similar to the buses operated in London by Thomas Tilling. They were registered O 8200–8212. The first three (O 8200–8202) arrived in Birmingham on 25 April 1912 and entered service a month later. By November 1912 the company were running a total of thirteen vehicles.

Further buses followed in 1913; this time they were Tilling-Stevens TTA2, which had conventionally placed front-mounted radiators and more powerful Tilling-Stevens 40-hp engine. These double-deckers were registered O 9913–9936, and all entered service between February and April 1913. One more Tilling-Stevens TTA2 double-decker arrived, registered OA 2549. By June of that year, motorbuses were running on all the company's routes and only seventeen horse buses remained in use on the Warwick Road service. The first twenty of the buses, O 8200–12 and O 9913–9919, were bought by the Birmingham District Power & Traction Co. and transferred to BMMO by a transfer of shares. The rest of these early Tilling-Stevens vehicles were legally always owned by the BDP&T and were hired to BMMO until their transfer to the Corporation on 4 October 1914.

On 5 September 1913, Birmingham Corporation opened its new tramway route along Hagley Road and, under the conditions imposed by the Watch Committee, the BMMO was obliged to withdraw its motorbuses from that route. The residents of Hagley Road, which bordered the exclusive Calthorpe Estate, had vehemently protested at the introduction of electric tramcars. An attempt to placate the anti-tram residents was made by the introduction of a short-lived First Class service in February 1914. The Hagley Road tram route gradually took commuters off the railway but, within a few years, Hagley Road had numerous motorbus services over-running the tram service, resulting in the Hagley Road tram service losing money. As a result the trams were withdrawn by Birmingham Corporation in 9 September 1930 and the passenger services on the Harborne Railway ended on 26 November 1934.

Hostility from the Corporation meant that BMMO was going to find it extremely difficult to expand its network of motorbus services within the city. Birmingham Corporation had already consolidated its role as virtually the sole operator of trams as early as 1907 and, in February 1914, BMMO and the Corporation signed an agreement about bus operation, allowing the company to operate services into the city centre from places outside the boundary subject to protective fares being charged. This trendsetting and statesman-like 'Birmingham Agreement' protected municipal transport services within the city, with profits going into the rates account, while enabling BMMO to operate buses beyond the city boundary and yet gain access to the city centre.

As part of the agreement, the leasehold on the Tennant Street Garage was transferred to Birmingham Corporation along with the services inside the Birmingham boundary. The first thirty of the BMMO Tilling-Stevens buses were transferred to the BCT fleet and were numbered 0–29. The agreement and transfer to BCT was finally implemented on 4 October 1914. BMMO moved to Bearwood, from where it pioneered countrywide bus services radiating from Birmingham. The first such service commenced on 24 December 1913 to Walsall and, throughout 1914, other services were introduced. On 28 February 1914, a service from Birmingham to Coventry, through Yardley, was inaugurated and by the summer of 1914 routes to Redditch, Kidderminster, Stourbridge, Evesham, Stratford, Warwick, Worcester and Great Malvern were being operated.

Until the early 1920s, most of the buses bought new by the company were Tilling-Stevens petrol-electrics and, with the exception of second-hand buses acquired from operators taken over by Midland Red, all were single-deckers. In 1915 two Tilling-Stevens TTA2s chassis were acquired, fitted with double-deck bodies and registered OA 7100 and OA 7101. In February 1918, the North Warwickshire Motor Omnibus & Transport Co. of Tamworth was taken over, along with four of their eight surviving Tilling-Stevens chassis with double-deck bodies. AC 32 was a TTA2 model, while AC 26, 33 and 43 were the later TS3 model. All these early petrol-electric Tilling-Stevens double-deckers had been scrapped by about 1920. This meant that the Midland Red company had no double-deckers in service for the first time since the company had been formed and it would be another two years before they were reintroduced to the fleet.

(0–12)
Overleaf above: Between 1912 and 1914, BMMO not only began services within Birmingham but also expanded into the Black Country, which quickly became the company's operational heartland. While still being operated by BMMO, this unidentified thirty-four-seater Tilling-Stevens TTA1 petrol-electric bus stands in Oldbury Market Place behind a hansom cab while waiting to return to Smethwick by way of Langley; the bus has a Renault-style bonnet with the radiator mounted behind the engine. This bus was transferred to Birmingham Corporation on 4 October 1914. Behind the railings are Oldbury's stylish red brick Municipal Buildings, built in 1890. (T. Daniels collection)

10, O 8210

O 8210 entered service in October 1912 as one of the thirteen Tilling-Stevens TTA1 petrol-electrics used in Midland Red's second attempt to use motorbuses on the Broad Street/ Five Ways and either Hagley Road or Harborne routes. O8210 is standing in Bearwood with its crew and inspector posing alongside the double-decker. These 30-hp buses had petrol-electric transmission with the engine driving an electric dynamo, which in turn drove the back axle. The buses had a distinctly continental look, its radiator being mounted on the driver's bulkhead with a stylish Renault coal scuttle bonnet. (Commercial Postcard)

13, O 9913, 17, O 9917

A pair of brand-new BMMO-owned 40-hp Tilling-Stevens TTA2s petrol-electrics – the front one, O 9913, being the first of the batch – stands at the Harborne terminus in the shadow of the Duke of York Public House at the stop near the corner of Serpentine Road in the early spring of 1913. This bus has the original style of radiator header tank badge, whereas the one behind carries the more common 'TILLING-STEVENS' lettering. The second bus is (O 9917), which is waiting for the crew of O 9913 to finish posing for the photographer before driving back to New Street by way of Five Ways and Broad Street. Both buses have a single headlight rather unusually mounted on the canopy above the driver. (D. R. Harvey collection)

23, O 9923

Fully laden for the benefit of the photographer, O 9923 is parked alongside the stone wall of a farmhouse in Hagley Road, which is selling home-produced milk at the kitchen door. The sign for the milk is just visible. The bus is a Tilling-Stevens TTA2 petrol-electric with a Tilling O18/16RO body. It entered service in March 1913 and was transferred to Birmingham Corporation on 5 October 1914. The bus had a long life for those days, not being withdrawn until 5 December 1924, having been used on the Selly Oak–Northfield bus service before the Bristol Road tramway was extended. (Whitcombe collection)

25, O 9925

What appears to be an engine adjustment has just been completed on O 9925. The bus is in Halesowen Street, Blackheath, and is working on the service outside the Birmingham boundary to Quinton during 1913. The bus is a Tilling-Stevens TTA2 with petrol-electric transmission and Tilling O18/16RO body, and would survive until November 1924 after its sale to Birmingham Corporation ten years earlier. (D. R. Harvey collection)

AC 26

Originally built for the Nuneaton & Stockingford Petrol Omnibus Co. in 1914 is Warwickshire-registered Tilling-Stevens TS3 petrol-electric double-decker AC 26, pictured in Nuneaton when new. It proudly proclaims what it is and who owns it on its side panels. When it was acquired by BMMO in 1918 it was re-registered O 9933. In 1920 it was re-registered again as OA 343 and in 1924 converted to forward control as a Tilling-Stevens FS and fitted with a new Carlyle O22/29F body. It lasted until 1928! (D. R. Harvey collection)

The FS Double-Deckers, 1922-1929

In 1922 Mr Shire designed a double-deck body that was fitted to OE 3151, a former War Department Tilling-Stevens TS3 lorry built in 1919 and then type designated FS. The engine was the standard TS3 four-cylinder side-valve 4.344-litre petrol engine, but was fitted with modified Ricardo cylinder heads, which improved their performance; as such, it was known as the BMMO 'Wonder' engine. They were still fitted with the easy-to-drive petrol-electric transmission, whose Achilles' heel was a somewhat gutless performance and a disappointing fuel economy. The Carlyle O22/29F body was little more than the standard single-decker with an open–top upper saloon and knifeboard seating added to it. Unusually it had a forward entrance and a rear-facing front staircase. The chassis was basically a single-decker converted to forward control with a very exposed open cab for the driver; this was soon altered to have a totally enclosed cab. This bus proved to be a prototype for a further fifty-five FS double-deckers.

Later in 1922 the first production batch of semi-forward control Tilling-Stevens FS chassis was placed in service as OK 1237–1241 and were followed in 1923 by HA 2242–2256 and HA 2257–76 in 1924. In addition, another fifteen earlier TS3 chassis were converted to forward control and fitted with new Carlyle O22/29F bodies. These were the former single-deckers OA 343–346 and 348, of 1913 vintage; a 1914 Tilling-Stevens TS3 chassis, registered OA 4555 and rebodied in 1923; and a 1915 chassis, also rebodied in 1923, registered OA 7090–96 and 7098–99. The buses were 25 feet 4½ inches long and had a 15⁵⁄₁₆-inch wheelbase. These buses, although still officially Tilling-Stevens chassis, were the immediate predecessors to Mr Shire's own buses that were built to his specification. Thus, the SOS marque was born, with the letters standing for 'Shire's Own Specification'.

Although fairly primitive to look at, what was amazing was that the FS double-deckers were operated on long journeys from Birmingham to Coventry and on the Coventry–Leamington Spa service. A large quantity of the FS double-deckers were used for the increasing number of Leicester town services yet, despite their extensive use for six years, all were withdrawn between 1928 and 1929 and the company reverted to only operating single-deck buses.

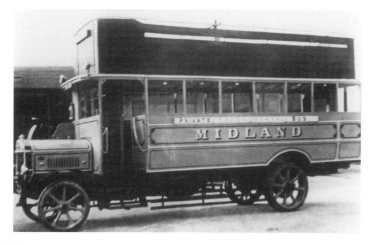

122 OE 3151

Parked in Carlyle Road Works yard is the prototype of the fifty-six-strong FS class of double-deckers, originally built as a normal control Tilling-Stevens TS3 chassis for the War Department, where it had been used as a lorry. It was bought as part of a job lot of twenty-one vehicles by BMMO. Its chassis number 947 suggests it was new about 1916 and was finally registered OE 3151, a mark used before in 1919. In 1920 it was converted to forward control with a totally unprotected cab in front of the forward entrance and an open top body looking like a single-decker with a deep protective cage around the roof edge. It was later fitted with an enclosed cab, which looked as if it had been nailed on as an afterthought. (BMMO)

210, OK 1239

Parked in Angel Place, Worcester, in 1923 are two of Midland Red's Tilling-Stevens FS double-deckers and two single-deck buses. The nearest bus is OK 1239, working on the 25 route to Malvern service, having not long arrived from Birmingham. In front of it is OA 4574, a 1914 single-deck Tilling-Stevens TS3, rebodied in 1919 with a new Tilling B29F body; it is waiting to go to Pershore on route 35. The distant double-decker is another Tilling-Stevens FS, OA 4555, also rebuilt to a forward-entrance fifty-one-seater in 1923. Despite looking both imposing and frail at the same time, it is being used on the long route to Birmingham by way of Droitwich, Bromsgrove and Rednal, where it will cross the Birmingham City boundary and use Bristol Road in order to reach its Worcester Street terminus. (A. G. Jenson)

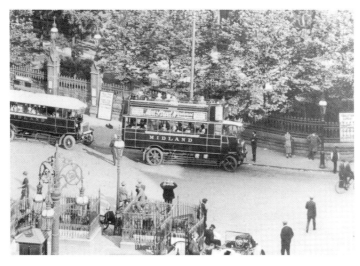

330, HA 2243

HA 2243, one of Midland Red's 1922 forward-control Tilling-Stevens open-top double-deckers, but with front entrance and staircase, is parked in the Bull Ring in Birmingham in front of St Martin's Parish Church, which was one of the main termini for long-distance bus services from Birmingham. The bus is being used on the service to Worcester, but the FS vehicles were also employed on routes to Coventry and Walsall. These buses had knifeboard seating with longitudinal benches placed back-to-back on the crown of the 'camel-back' arch to the lower saloon roof. This seating arrangement was used to reduce height and to lessen the chances of passengers being struck by tree-branches on country routes. To protect female modesty, the advertisement panels or 'decency boards' were very high but resulted in the view from the top deck being rather restricted. (D. R. Harvey collection)

379, HA 2261

Manoeuvring over the railway bridge near Bedworth in Coventry Road, Nuneaton is HA 2261. The Carlyle-built O22/29F body was quite advanced for its day, having both an enclosed driver's cab and passenger staircase. This was one of the last FS type double-deckers to be constructed in 1924 but was withdrawn in 1928 when all the FS buses were phased out. It would be another three years before the next generation of SOS double-deckers would be introduced. (D. R. Harvey collection)

1931–1934: SOS REDDs

The heart of Midland Red's operating domain was to the west of Birmingham in the heavily industrialised Black Country. The Midland Red fleet had been wholly single-decker for two years before the need for a new double-decker became a necessity after all the company tram routes in the Black Country had been abandoned.

The model produced at Carlyle Road in 1931 was Midland Red's first modern double-deck chassis. Originally designated DD, this was quickly altered to REDD (Rear Entrance Double-Decker). In 1931, a modified version of the IM6 single-decker chassis was constructed, but with a much shorter 15-foot 7-inch long wheelbase to suit a double-deck body. The prototype double-decker body was built on SOS chassis 1541. It was registered HA 7329 and given the BMMO 'A' fleet number 1319. It had cost £1,770 to build, which was about double the price of the contemporary IM4 or IM6 single-decker. HA 7329 had a drop frame rear extension for a rear platform and was 25 feet 3 inches long. It was fitted with the RR 2 LB 6.373-litre petrol engine and one of the newly introduced 'silent third' gearboxes, which was designed to take the extra torque of the larger engines.

The complete bus was bodied to Midland Red requirements by Short Brothers of Rochester in Kent.

The odd-looking six-bay construction body had a seating split of twenty-six downstairs but only twenty-two in the upper saloon. The upper saloon stopped level with the lower saloon front bulkhead. A raked apron below the front of the upper saloon was slightly V-shaped and was devoid of any destination equipment. This strange front profile reduced the unladen weight complying with the current legislation on 26-foot-long double-deckers and, although HA 7329 weighed in at 6½ tons, in order to pass the compulsory tilt-test many coachbuilders did not build over the cab. There was an emergency exit in the lower saloon in the first off-side bay, as the cut-away on the rear platform appeared not to conform to the latest Construction and Use Regulations. The rest of the body design was up to date, with matching styles of glazing for both the platform and upper saloon emergency window. This first REDD was extensively rebuilt in 1937. As the first of its kind, HA 7329 operated alongside many SOS prototypes from Bearwood Garage, moving to Leicester in 1939. It came back to Bearwood Garage in December 1946 and outlived the even uglier prototype FEDD by surviving until 1948.

In 1932, a block of fifty Smethwick HA registrations were reserved. The HA marks had been the characteristic of Midland Red since being first used in 1922. Now, the company booked a consecutive batch of numbers for the new production batch of REDDs. These were HA 8001–8050, although one of the batch, HA 8002, was never operated and was transferred to Northern General, and was rebodied by Northern Coach Builders in 1945 with a modern-looking H30/26R body. It was withdrawn in 1952.

The production batch of these fifty REDDs was distinctly different from the prototype vehicle. They were built to an overall length of 25 feet 11 inches; as a result the wheelbase length was increased to 16 feet 1½ inches. They had the same RR2 LB (long bore), 6.373-litre, six-cylinder, side-valve engine as the prototype and retained the 'silent third; helical spur gearbox. The braking performance of the REDDs was 'uninspired' and of course the poor driver dare not stall his charge, as he would have to 'wind-it by hand' as there self-starters were not fitted!

The Midland Red REDDs were all highbridge buses, and were built to an H26/26R format – four more than that on HA 7329. The body contract for these Midland Red REDDs was awarded to four different body builders. These were Brush, Eastern Counties, Short Brothers and Metro-Cammell. The registration numbers were allocated in consecutive blocks to each bodybuilder and not by fleet number. The chassis numbers were between 1623 and 1676.

Short Brothers built the first fifteen, HA 8001–8015, which began to enter service in October 1932. Eastern Counties built the next ten, HA 8016–8025, which were the only bodies built by ECOC on SOS double-decker chassis. The next fifteen were bodied by Brush, who were Midland Red's regular body builder, and were registered HA 8026–8040; like all the others the registration numbers were in the correct sequence in relation to the scattered fleet numbers. The final batch of ten had metal-framed Metro-Cammell bodies and were registered HA 8041–8050. Surprisingly all the BMMO production buses were lighter than the prototype HA 7329, weighing between 6 tons 6 cwt and 6 tons 8 cwt. The bodies had a 'semi-piano' front design with a very short front upper saloon bay with a gentle double-curve down to the top of the driver's cab. While conforming to the specifications of Midland Red, all four body builders produced variations that could be easily distinguished.

All the compositely bodied Midland Red REDDs were initially operated in the Birmingham and Black Country area, while the ten Metro-Cammell-bodied examples went straight to Leicester, thus reintroducing Midland Red double-deckers once more to the city. Both Digbeth and Dudley garages had some when they were new, while Bearwood's allocation was taken from the Short-bodied REDDs. Just prior to the outbreak of war, all forty-one of the Birmingham area REDDs, including the prototype, were transferred to the Leicester area. It was during their sojourn in Leicester that their seating capacity was increased to fifty-five, with an increase of three in the upper saloon making them H29/26R. In the twilight of their operating lives, about half of the REDDs returned to the Birmingham area. Withdrawals began in 1948 and the last six survived into 1951.

The only other batch REDDs to be built had chassis numbers 1926–1940/46 and were the last of the model to be built. They were delivered to Potteries Motor Traction and numbered 232–243 (AVT 552-563), which had Short L30/26R bodies, while 244-247 (AVT 564-567) had MCCW L26/26R bodies.

1319, HA 7329

HA 7329 is parked alongside the destination post for Kingswinford and Wolverhampton in Foster Street Bus Station in Stourbridge in about 1938, not long after it had a major chassis rebuild. This was the 1931 prototype SOS FEDD, which had a six-bay H22/26R body built by Short Brothers with a somewhat eccentrically styled piano front. This was built in this style in order to comply with the very stringent front-axle weight regulations. The cab area reveals its modified single-deck origins, with the petrol tank fitted beneath the driver's seat in the standard Midland Red manner, but the rest of the bodywork looks remarkably up to date. (R. Wilson)

1371, HA 8016

Standing at the Barley Mow in Solihull on 8 May 1949 is 1371, HA 8016. This SOS REDD has an ECOC H26/26R body and appears in a very smart condition despite being seventeen years old and only about one year away from withdrawal. It is working on a well-subscribed 155 service from the Bull Ring in Birmingham to Station Road, Knowle, a journey timed at 38 minutes. (J. Cull)

1372, HA 8026

The allocation of fleet numbers in March 1944 based on the Private Identification Numbers of the fifty Midland Red REDDs at first sight seems very strange; however, a kind of logic was to be found in their Midland Red BB body numbers, with HA 8026 being the first of the Brush body sequence BB2009–2023. 1372 is at the bus shelters opposite the King's Head Public House in Hagley Road, Bearwood, when working on a heavily loaded 140 service from Dudley to Birmingham via Blackheath. (D. R. Harvey collection)

1410, HA 8036

Just before the outbreak of the Second World War, most of the Brush-bodied REDDs were transferred away from the West Midlands to operate in the Leicester area. They had been largely replaced by the FHA-registered SOS FEDDs in the Black Country. HA 8036 is about to work on a service to Wigston on 10 July 1939. These fifteen 1932-vintage Brush-bodied REDDs had the best styled curved front profiles of all these double-deckers. Behind it is a four-years-newer DHA-registered SON with an English Electric body. (J. Cull)

1377, HA 8004

Left: The driver of Short-bodied SOS REDD 1377, HA 8004, must have been a tram driver in a previous life as he has not made any allowances for the women who have to walk in the road in order to get onto the bus. 1377 is in Aylestone Road on a misty 27 January 1945. Behind the bus is Leicester City Transport's tram 13. This much-rebuilt ERT & CW-bodied tram, mounted on Brill 21E trucks, dated from 1904 and would survive until 1948. (First Leicester)

1380, HA 8005

Below: Speeding along Oldbury Road and passing the former West Smethwick tram depot entrance in about 1947 is HA 8005. This SOS REDD, by now numbered 1380, was bodied by Short Brothers, who had bodied the prototype REDD. Bodywork on production REDDs was of five-bay construction rather than the six of the prototype. Also, the offside lower saloon emergency exit had been eliminated. The bus is on the very busy route B87 from Birmingham to Dudley by way of Smethwick and Oldbury. (A. N. Porter)

1391, HA 8048

Right: The cab windows were considerably higher than the lower saloon windows and, coupled with narrow offset cab, it made the driver's position look cramped and somewhat perched. 1391, HA 8048, is in Navigation Street in Birmingham on 15 October 1949 and is working on the 140 service. This bus had a MCCW H26/26R body and, as with all the REDDs, was fitted with the RR 2 LB 6.373-litre six-cylinder petrol engine and the 'silent third' gearbox, producing a lively performance. (J. Cull)

1412, HA 8044

Below: The MCCW-bodied REDDs had metal-framed bodies, which could be distinguished from the other composite bodies by their lack of any radius to the saloon windows. 1412, HA 8044, stands in Humberstone Gate, Leicester, awaiting its next duty in about 1947. It carries an early post-war advertisement for Crosse & Blackwell's soups, an old purveyor of foods originally dating from 1706. The bus would remain in service until 1951. (S. N. J. White)

1933–1939: SOS FEDD

Although the fifty REDDs of 1932 and 1933 had been a qualified success, something more modern and perhaps more eye-catching was required for future double-deckers. A return to a front entrance body yet again became an attractive proposition to the Midland Red operation's staff, and during 1933 the SOS FEDD (Front Entrance Double-Decker) was developed specifically for the needs of Midland Red's ever-increasing intensive urban services, especially in the Black Country and the Leicester area. The mechanical specification of the new double-decker bus was very similar to that of the previous REDD design. It had the same SOS RR2 LB six-cylinder side-valve petrol engine of 6.373 litres and a 'silent third' gearbox, but the wheelbase on the FEDD was increased by 1 inches to 16 feet 3¼ inches. The prototype was registered HA 9000 and built on SOS chassis 1727. It was allocated the BMMO A number 1448 in 1944, though at first it briefly carried the number 1000.

The ungainly Carlyle-built H26/26F body was even more eccentric than that on the prototype REDD of 1931. The body had a large open porch entrance with a rear ascending front staircase opposite the doorway. The rear of the body was very similar to the later production FEDDs; however, as a weight-reducing measure, the ungainly upper saloon stopped short of the lower saloon front bulkhead with the front panel design between the decks similar to the design of the REDD bodies, although it incorporated a destination roller blind beneath a triple route number stencil holder. The whole effect was more like a 1920s double deck body with a flat exposed roof above the driver's cab. The radiator was also unique in that it was raked backwards and fitted with a nearside bicycle front wing that was little more than a single curved metal sheet. Incredibly the bus weighed only 5 tons 14 cwt and, at only 13 feet 11 inches tall, it could get under most low bridges. HA 9000 spent all of its life working from Bearwood Garage on Birmingham and Black Country services and was withdrawn in 1947, a year before the prototype REDD 1319 (HA 7329), but it was not broken up until 1949.

The 1934 Fifty Short Brothers-Bodied FEDDs

In 1934, fifty composite Short Brothers H30/26F-bodied FEDDs with chassis numbers 1876–1925 had been ordered. These were the first production FEDDs and, at 25 feet 11¼ inches, were 2 inches longer than HA 9000. As a result of the revised body design, the Short-bodied FEDDs weighed 6 tons 3 cwt. These first fifty buses were registered HA 9401–9450 and received the 'A' numbers 1536–1586 in the Midland Red fleet in 1944. Midland Red had become an important customer for the Rochester-based company, who would provide some 325 bodies between 1930 and 1935, and so ordering Short Brothers bodies was only following the Midland Red policy at the time.

The Short-bodied SOS FEDDS differed from the prototype in having the upper saloon extended over the driver's cab, although there was a slight curve at the bottom of the front panel above the driver's cab. This shape was repeated on the subsequent solitary English Electric body, HA 9432, and the 135 Midland Red and fifteen Trent Metro-Cammell-bodied examples of 1935 and 1936. The fifty Short-bodied vehicles were equipped with a large sliding external front door operated by the conductor and had their seating increased from the prototype by four to a H30/26F layout. The buses were delivered in gold lined-out red with two cream livery bands, a silver-painted roof and black mudguards. The Short-bodied FEDDS were particularly associated with Sutton Coldfield Garage, which in the late 1930s had almost half of these HA-registered FEDDS, while Digbeth and Oldbury garages had most of the remaining fifty buses.

There were some modifications to this batch of Short-bodied SOS FEDDS. 1566 (HA 9431) entered service in 1934 with the prototype BMMO K type 8.028-litre oil engine and, as a result of the increased weight of the diesel engine, the bus had a reduced H28/26F seating capacity. This engine was transferred to 1579 (HA 9444) in 1937. During 1944, 1542 (HA 9407) ran on producer gas from Kidderminster Garage but, as with most of these buses equipped with this emergency wartime method of propulsion, the bus was quickly returned to normal petrol operation as the side-valve BMMO petrol engine was very difficult to convert to producer gas operation. The somewhat angular Short bodies were robust but, in 1948, six buses were rebuilt by Samlesbury Engineering, while two more were rebuilt at Kegworth by Nudd Brothers and Lockyer in 1949. These eight buses were to be the last survivors of the Short-bodied FEDDS, being taken out of service in 1953. Withdrawals began in 1947 with 1555, which had been an accident victim, and all but nine of the Short-bodied FEDDS went by 1950.

The One-Off Body

1567 (HA 9432), one of the Short bodied FEDDS, was rebodied with the one-off new English Electric body in 1936, thus providing a float body. English Electric were to become a regular supplier of bodies to Midland Red from 1936 until 1938 but, despite the cost of producing a one-off speculative body, the one on 1567 was the only double-decker supplied by English Electric to Midland Red. Weighing just under 6½ tons, this bus remained in service until 1950, becoming the first FEDD to be withdrawn.

The Metro-Cammell Metal-Framed FEDD of 1936

The next order of SOS FEDDS was in two consecutive batches. Using their A numbers for ease of identification, they were 1742–1841 (BHA 301–400), which were not registered in order, and 1842–1876, which were BHA 801–835. The original order was for 150 FEDDS to be delivered in 1936, although two vehicles, 1743 and 1744, were delivered in December 1935. The body order was placed with Metro-Cammell but, unlike the previous orders, these were metal-framed. They had an H30/26R seating capacity and superficially looked like the Short-bodied FEDDs, having the attractive concave front panelling above the driver's cab and retaining the sliding front entrance door. Having metal-framed bodies, the Metro-Cammell FEDDs weighed 6 tons 14 cwt, which ensured a durability that meant that none of these buses required major rebuilding during their long lives. BHA 309 was the only one of the class to have a noticeably different body, having a lightweight pop-rivet body.

The way in which the buses were delivered was a little complex, as Trent Motor Traction, who had purchased ninety-four SOS ON and DON single-deckers between 1934 and 1936, were short of double-deckers. The chassis numbers of these buses was in the 2134 to 2233 range, with 2141/51/61–62/68–71/73–79 going to Trent. As a result, the last fifteen of the first order of 100 MCCW-bodied SOS FEDDs were transferred to fellow BET company Trent. These buses took the Trent fleet numbers 1000–1014 (RC 3322–3336) and were the only SOS double-deckers purchased by the company. This sale left Midland Red short of fifteen chassis and so, for delivery later in 1936, another fifty Metro-Cammell-bodied FEDDs were built, with the chassis numbers 2280–2329. Confusingly these were registered BHA 386–400 (1827–1841), which took over the A Numbers and registrations of those vehicles sold to Trent. The remaining thirty-five buses were registered BHA 801–835 and given the A Numbers 1842–1872 in March 1944, when the whole fleet received fleet numbers.

Of all the BHA-registered SOS FEDDs, only BHA 345 entered service with an AEC 7.57-litre oil engine, which it retained for two years before reverting to a standard BMMO petrol engine. When diesel-powered, in order to save weight, the bus's seating capacity was reduced to fifty-four by the omission of two upper saloon seats. Change was afoot and, between 1942 and 1947, all the BHA FEDDs were fitted with oil engines but the seating capacity was not altered. Ninety-five of the buses received BMMO K-type oil engines, while forty were re-engined with AEC 7.57-litre units.

Of the initial allocation of the MCCW-bodied FEDDs, over sixty, including all of the BHA 801–835 registered vehicles, were allocated to Digbeth Garage for the routes out to Stratford and Coventry. Those allocated to the Black Country garages had a much harder time slogging up steep hills on frequently indifferent road surfaces. BHA 331–355 were delivered new to Dudley Garage and nearby Harts Hill had twenty-five FEDDs. Both Oldbury and Stourbridge also had a small batch of BHA FEDDs in 1936.

Outside the West Midlands, Sandacre Street in Leicester had always had a fairly large number of these Metro-Cammell-bodied FEDDs for the Leicester City services, while Stafford Garage also had some for their town services. Other BHA FEDDs were at Redditch and Stourbridge, and those allocated to Sutton Coldfield were the first double-deckers in the town since the local council lifted its ban.

Withdrawals began in 1953, when fifty of the buses were taken out of service, while in 1954 another fifty-one went for scrap. The following year twenty-three were taken out of service, leaving just eleven of the class running at the start of 1956. The last three of the MCCW-bodied FEDDs, 1756, 1807 and 1865, were withdrawn at the tender age of twenty-one years old in 1957.

The First Brush-Bodied FEDDs: Fifty EHA-Registered Buses

The next fifty FEDDs were ordered in 1937 for delivery in the first half of 1938 and were distinctly different from the previous buses. The chassis were built with the SOS K type six-cylinder oil engine of 8.028 litres. All subsequent FEDDs were equipped with this engine and were coupled to the very advanced German-made ZF Aphon four-speed gearbox. This gearbox had helical gears on the intermediate ratios and was virtually silent in its operation; it was apparently so easy to use that many drivers were able to change gear without using the clutch.

Again the order for the bodywork went to another coachbuilder, this time Brush. Their first batch of fifty, the 1938 series composite construction FEDDs, were registered EHA 251–300, becoming fleet numbers 2119–2168 in 1944. The front profile of these buses eliminated the step between the top of the lower saloon above the cab and the upper saloon, while the small front upper saloon side windows had a heavily radiused front lower curve, similar to the contemporary Brush bodies being supplied to Coventry Corporation. The whole appearance of the Brush product was more rounded than either of the previous Short or Metro-Cammell body designs, with the front entrance altered to a porch with the usual two steps up into the saloon and jack-knife doors, which had a paired opening arrangement so that the conductor could just pull on one of the doors and both would open. The interior of both saloons was fitted with yellow, brown and gold moquette with the body pillars capped in dark painted wood and black vertical stanchions. The only jarring note was that the upper saloon still had a single-skinned roof, which was the standard layout until the end of FEDD production in the autumn of 1939. EHA 251–300 were also unique among all the FEDD classes as they had their fuel tanks located on the offside at chassis level rather than beneath the driver's cab seat, as had been the normal, if somewhat quirky habit on pre-war SOS double- and single-decker chassis. This arrangement also meant that the offside cab window was longer and that the driver's door was also wider. The subsequent final two batches of FEDDs reverted to the fuel tank being placed beneath the driver's seat.

Four of the buses, EHA 251, 290, 292 and 298, were fitted with a new style of chromed radiator. The previous style was a very plain affair, with a plate with a concave-shaped header tank emboldened with the word 'MIDLAND' and a thin central vertical bar with the legend 'SOS'. The new radiator had a much thicker polished edge and a triangular top with a large SOS badge vaguely resembling the radiators on AEC vehicles. This style of radiator was fitted to the rest of the EHA-registered FEDDs retrospectively. At the end of the Second World War the large triangular SOS batch was replaced by a similarly styled badge, but with the letters 'BMMO' embossed onto it, thus burying the SOS marque of Mr Wyndham Shire under the new regime of Mr Donald Sinclair. Three of these four buses, EHA 290, 292 and 298, later to become 2158, 2160 and 2165, were equipped with full-front cabs from new, but were converted to the normal half-cab arrangement in 1940, although retaining their original wider windscreens. In October 1942, 2167 (EHA 299) was rebuilt with a curved, somewhat drooping set of front and side upper saloon windows. A concealed radiator was also fitted, serving as the trial design for the prototype D1, HHA 1. 2254 (FHA 236) ran with a lightweight 'S. & B.' body, which meant 'skin and bones'.

All fifty of the EHA-registered FEDDs were rebuilt by Aero-Engineering & Marine (Merseyside) at the RAF's 610 Auxiliary Squadron airfield at Hooton Park. This company was better known as 'Hooton'. The rebuilding, necessitated by the rigours of wartime operating conditions on the Brush composite construction bodies, resulted in new framing as well as most noticeably rubber-mounted saloon windows. Some bodies were considered to be in sufficiently good condition that they only had one saloon rebuilt, this usually being the lower saloon. This rebuilding process began in 1949, when two bodies were rebuilt, and was completed in 1951 with the final twenty-five.

The allocation of the EHA-registered FEDDS was somewhat scattered across the company's operating area, though generally they were found at garages in urban areas. A number of the EHA-registered FEDDS were allocated to Digbeth Garage when new and some stayed throughout their careers. The overspill garage at Sheepcote Street, Birmingham, which opened with an allocation of seventy buses in 1951 had some of the 2119–2168 vehicles until their final withdrawal in 1960. In the Black Country, Oldbury Garage had a small batch while at Stourbridge Garage there were usually a handful of the EHA vehicles, as there were at Dudley. Bromsgrove Garage had about a dozen FEDDs and, in the post-war period, both Kidderminster and Redditch garages had small allocations of EHA-registered FEDDs. During 1950, Leicester's Southgate Street had a few of these buses after the withdrawal of their SOS REDDs. Finally the small number at Emscote Garage, Warwick, were transferred in September 1957 to the new Myton Road premises in Leamington. Withdrawals commenced in 1956 and were completed in 1960, when the final nine were taken out of service, though 2120 lingered on as a staff bus until 1961.

The FHA 2xx Batch of 1938/1939

Another fifty Brush-bodied FEDDs concluded the rest of 1938 programme. These buses reverted to having the fuel tank beneath the driver's seat and the original offside, fussy-looking three-cab-window arrangement with the narrow cab door. Other than this, these buses were virtually the same as the EHA-registered buses, though all were equipped from new with the new, more attractively designed radiator. The buses were registered FHA 201–221, 200, 223–250 and were given the A numbers in 1944 of 2219–2268. 2219–2227 entered service in 1938, while 2228–2268 arrived in 1939. The missing registration FHA 222 was allocated, apparently in error, to a Smethwick Fire Brigade engine and so FHA 200 was substituted.

Like the first fifty Brush-bodied FEDDs, the composite bodies were in need of rebuilding after about ten years of service. As a result, 2235 (FHA 217) was given the prototype body rebuild by the company at Carlyle Road Works. The remaining forty-nine vehicles were rebuilt between 1949 and 1951 by Aero-Engineering & Marine (Merseyside), as with the EHA buses.

Many of these buses spent most of their lives in the Birmingham and Black Country area, being allocated to Digbeth and Sheepcote Street in Birmingham, Bearwood, Brierley Hill, Dudley and Sutton Coldfield garages. Elsewhere, Leicester's Sandacre Street had a number of this batch of buses, which stayed for eighteen years, while at the very end of their lives a small quantity were allocated to Myton Road, Leamington. In the 1950s, there was also a small fleet allocated to Stafford for the town services.

Withdrawals began in 1956 when five vehicles, 2235, 2241, 2246, 2248 and 2263, were taken out of service. By 1960 there were sixteen left and the final three, 2219, 2228 and 2254, were withdrawn in December 1960, though 2243 and 2261 ran as training buses for another year.

The FHA 8xx Batch of the Autumn of 1939

The final batch of fifty SOS FEDDs were registered FHA 836–885 in the autumn of 1939 and in 1944 were given the fleet numbers 2332–2381. Bodied again by Brush of Loughborough with the H30/26F layout, the body design was even more rounded with a deep roof line and a heavily curved rear dome. The rear side windows in the rear dome were almost D-shaped, mirrored by similarly shaped rear side windows in the lower saloon. This body styling by Brush would be reflected on the final 1940 batch of SOS SON single-deckers. The entire batch of the FHA 8xx series of Brush-bodied SOS FEDDs were allocated to Oldbury Garage in order to operate on the B87 service from Birmingham to Dudley via Smethwick and Oldbury after Birmingham City Transport abandoned the Dudley Road tram services, known as 'The Track', on 30 September 1939. By the mid-1950s, half of the class were still at Oldbury; they were gradually displaced by BMMO D7s and even the first of the BMMO D9s.

There were a number of modifications to this batch of vehicles. In 1940 FHA 868 received experimental Dunlop heavy-duty rubber front wings and was subsequently modified with a sliding window behind the driver in order that it might be used by Bearwood Garage's driver training school. FHA 841 had an electric bell system, which replaced the cord-pulls in the lower saloon; FHA 845 had an unspecified experimental clutch; and FHA 856 ran for a time with a Lockheed braking system, while FHA 870 was equipped with air-brakes.

Again the Brush bodies were in need of renovation after the Second World War. The pilot rebuild was undertaken by Carlyle in 1950 with the body of 2337, while that on 2341 was uniquely the only Brush-bodied FEDD to be rebuilt by Nudd Brothers & Lockyer at Kegworth, which they also undertook in 1950. The remaining forty-eight of these last-ever FEDDs were rebuilt by Aero-Engineering & Marine at Hooton, with twenty-nine being rebuilt in 1950 and the last nineteen during the following year. Withdrawals began in 1957, when fifteen buses were taken out of service and sixteen continued operating until 1960. The final three, 2358, 2372 and 2381, were retired in December 1960, with just one bus, 2370, surviving until 1961 as a driver training vehicle at Bearwood Garage.

There were 336 SOS FEDDs operated by Midland Red, with another fifteen being supplied to Trent Motor Traction. The indifferent roads in the Black Country played havoc with the suspension, and brake wear was extremely high on some of the fearsome hills in the Blackheath, Oldbury and Dudley area. Frequently carrying full loads, the Metro-Cammell metal-framed buses led a full life without the need for reconstruction, whereas the later composite bodies built by Brush did require heavy mid-life rebuilding. Yet, the FEDDs, with their medium-sized petrol and later oil engines and somewhat frail-looking lightweight bodies, served the company from 1933 until 1961 extraordinarily well on heavily subscribed urban services; it was a pity that one did not survive into the preservation era.

A strange coincidence is that the three types of Midland Red double-deckers to achieve prominence were produced in similar in numbers, with 351 pre-war SOS FEDDs, 350 BMMO D7s and 344 of the advanced D9s. Adding in the 200 D5 and D5B vehicles of 1949–1952, that is a total of 1,245 Midland Red-built buses. Not a bad total for just a bus operator!

1448, HA 9000
The prototype FEDD ('front-entrance double-decker') HA 9000 picks up passengers at the Scott Arms, when working on the Birmingham–Walsall service in 1938. It was a curious-looking front-entrance bus with the cycle-type front mudguards and an antique-looking frontal appearance with the top deck, fitted with front indicators, starting behind the front bulkhead, resulting in the cab projecting beyond the top deck. By contrast the rear profile was both modern and neat, being the only FEDD to have a full set of rear destination boxes. It spent most of its fifteen-year life allocated to Bearwood Garage, working on the 118 route to Walsall. (P. Tizard)

1536, HA 9401
The first production FEDD was 1536, HA 9401, which the first of the fifty composite construction Short-bodied buses. In 1936, this bus, beautifully painted in the two cream banded lined-out livery, is working on the long 144 route between Station Street in Birmingham and Malvern Wells via Bromsgrove, where it is picking up passengers, and Worcester, a journey that took 2 hours and 22 minutes. Its body would be one of only two to be rebuilt in 1949 by Nudd Bros & Lockyer. (D. R. Harvey collection)

1548, HA 9422

The lack of a rear destination box meant that a slip board beneath the rear emergency door had to be used. Fortunately HA 9422 is displaying one that shows that this Short-bodied SOS FEDD is working along Stratford Road in Hall Green on the Solihull service via the nearby Shirley. The bus is approaching the Robin Hood Cinema and, as the bus entered service in 1934 and the Corporation tram route on Stratford Road was abandoned on 7 January 1937, this dates the scene to 1936. In 1944, one of this batch, 1542, HA 9407, was the only SOS FEDD to be converted to run on producer gas. (Birmingham City Engineers)

1552, HA 9414

One of the last of the Short-bodied FEDDs in service was 1552, HA 9414. Exhibiting some evidence of rebuilding undertaken by Samlesbury in 1948, especially around the front of the upper saloon, the bus is parked at the Bridgefoot Bus Station in Stratford-upon-Avon with the Shakespeare Memorial Theatre alongside the River Avon in the distance. 1552 has just arrived in Stratford, having worked on the prestigious 150 service from Birmingham via Henley-in-Arden. (D. Simpson)

1565, HA 9430

The Priory Estate already been built across the Borough in the last decade, but was the largest council housing development in Dudley, being built to replace the town's early-nineteenth-century slums. The first houses were occupied in 1930 and, by the end of the decade, more than 2,000 houses had been built on the Priory and the nearby Wren's Nest estates. 1565, HA 9430, with a Short body stands at the Priory Estate terminus of the D1 service in Pine Road in about 1947, just beyond the end row of the council housing. This service ran every ten minutes and took only nine minutes from end to end. The bus has been restored to the fully lined-out post-war livery, though the attractive cream bands have by now been omitted. (D. R. Harvey collection)

1567, HA 9432

HA 9432 is at the English Electric factory in Preston, immediately prior to entering service in 1936. HA 9432 was originally a Short-bodied FEDD, but was rebodied with a one-off new composite-framed English Electric body in 1936, which, at first sight, could have been one of the slightly later Metro-Cammell bodies. This enabled HA 9432's original body to become available as a spare. English Electric was to become a regular supplier of bodies to Midland Red between 1936 and 1938 but, despite the cost of producing a one-off speculative body, the one on what later became 1567 was the only double-decker they ever supplied to Midland Red. Weighing just under 6½ tons, this bus remained in service until 1950. (EEC)

1744, BHA 301

The crew of the first Metro-Cammell-bodied SOS FEDD, 1744, BHA 301, take a break when working on the 611 from Kibworth to Leicester in about 1948. The radiator still retains its central chrome strip, which was generally removed after Mr Sinclair became the company's general manager. Standing behind a Vauxhall H Ten-Four saloon, the bus is in the early post-war livery, featuring a pre-war style silver roof. The bus entered service in 1935 and was taken out of service in 1953. The Metro-Cammell bodies were metal-framed and were long lasting in their original condition without the need for any reconstruction. (R. Hannay)

1758, BHA 316

Parked at Stand 5 in St Margaret's Bus Station, Leicester, alongside the Art Deco-styled concrete bus shelters is BHA 316. This MCCW-bodied SOS FEDD is working out of Leicester in about 1947 as the bus has the remains of the pre-war lining out and the BMMO garter on the cab apron. Beyond the bus station is Burley's Way with the Corah's 1940s hosiery factory away from that. The BHA FEDDs were all converted to oil engines with BHA 316 receiving an AEC 7.57-litre unit in 1943. It was given the fleet number 1758 in 1944 and stayed in service until 1954. (D. R. Harvey collection)

1791, BHA 335

Turning into New Street from High Street is 1791, BHA 335, working on 101 service to Streetly via the Erdington tram terminus at the Yenton Public House and the Parade in Sutton Coldfield. The bus is turning in front of the 'Big Top' site being used as a car park before redevelopment took place. This large corner site was destroyed in an air raid on 9 April 1941 and, once the site had been cleared at various times, it was used by a circus that had a big top tent. This MCCW H30/26F-bodied SOS FEDD, dating from 1935, has to its nearside 1750, BHA 308, another of the same batch. Meanwhile, sandwiched between them is an almost-new Birmingham City Transport bus, 2019, JOJ 19, a 1950 Daimler CVD6, also with a Metro-Cammell body, being used on the 29 route to Kingstanding. (D. R. Harvey collection)

1800, BHA 344

A gentleman with trilby hat and gabardine mackintosh is rushing for the bus in Stourbridge Bus Station in about 1949. This bus station was unusual in that part of the garage was also used for intending passengers. The man is about to board 1800 (BHA 344), one of the 1936 Metro-Cammell-bodied FEDDS on route 246 to Dudley via Amblecote and Brierley Hill, which had replaced the Dudley & Stourbridge tram service on 1 March 1930. The heavy sliding door was always opened and closed by the conductor, who must have had very well-developed biceps. The bus, despite receiving an AEC 7.57-litre oil engine in 1944, would be one of the early withdrawals of the BHA series in 1953. (M. Rooum)

1837, BHA 396

Right: Parked outside the thirteenth-century St Alphege Parish Church near to the Square in Solihull's High Street is the almost-new BHA 396, later to become 1837. The ornate lined-out red livery, with two cream bands and a silver roof, is a complete contrast to the drab all-over red it would receive after the Second World War. This Metro-Cammell-bodied SOS FEDD is soon to depart on the 154 service via Blossomfield Road, Stratford Road Shirley and Hall Green to terminate outside St Martin's Parish Church in Birmingham's Bull Ring. (J. Cull)

1853, BHA 812

Below: Travelling into New Street from Victoria Square in April 1944 is 1853, BHA 812. The provision of a rear destination box below the advertisement for Hovis is a welcome feature. Although the pedestrians all look well dressed, evidence of the privations of war are all too evident with white-painted street furniture, air raid sign posts and the direction notice to the YWCA Club. Even 1853, a MCCW-bodied SOS FEDD has its bottom rear corners painted in white to assist recognition in the blackout. (D. R. Harvey collection)

1855, BHA 814

BHA 814, a Metro-Cammell bodied FEDD, is in Acocks Green, working on the busy 184 route from Birmingham to Olton and Solihull via Warwick Road. The bus has been equipped with a nearside headlight mask and white blackout paint. That it still has the SOS badge on the radiator suggests that this was about 1940. The vestiges of a 'piano front' is there, with the curved front panel just below the front destination box. (J. C. Gillham)

1864, BHA 823

Awaiting its departure time in Newport Street bus station, Worcester, is 1864, BHA 823. In about 1948, this MCCW-bodied SOS FEDD is working on the 316 service to Stourbridge by way of Norton and Kidderminster, which took around 80 minutes. The bus has been painted in the early post-war all-over red livery with a white painted roof, but still retains some gold lining out. 1864 was converted to a BMMO 8.028-litre oil engine in 1944, which would have made it far more economical to operate. (R. Blencowe)

1874, BHA 833

1874, (BHA 833), one of the FEDDs with metal-framed MCCW bodies, stands under the advertisement hoardings in Navigation Street while working the 130 route to Stourbridge in May 1952. Hidden by the bus is the playbill for the Birmingham Hippodrome, where, for one week only, Stan Laurel and Oliver Hardy were top of the bill during their final successful tour of England. The bus was also in the twilight of its career and was destined to last only another three years. (S. N. J. White)

2120, EHA 252

At the very end of FEDD operation, within weeks of their ultimate demise, 2120 is parked outside Rudgeway House in Chester Road, Castle Bromwich, at 7.45 a.m. on 3 October 1960. It still has the original style of SOS radiator. By now twenty-two years old, this Brush-bodied FEDD looks in remarkably fine fettle as its crew prepare for the return journey to Birmingham. It shows that, although withdrawal was imminent, the last surviving FEDDs were kept on front-line duties until the end. (D. Johnson collection)

2135, EHA 267
The bodies on the EHA-registered batch of Brush SOS FEDDs abandoned the large, heavy sliding entrance door. This was replaced by a porch with a pair of doors at the top of the entrance steps. The conductor stands in the porch as 2135, (EHA 267), passes through Northampton Square at the end of Charles Street in Leicester when working on the L10 route to Wigston via Oadby in 1950. The composite Brush body had recently been renovated by Hooton with the lower saloon receiving rubber gasket mounted windows with sliding ventilators but those in the upper saloon being largely unaltered. (K. Lane)

2153, EHA 285
The driver and conductor enjoy their break when working on the on the 244 route to Cradley Heath during the Coronation celebrations of June 1953. 2153, (EHA 285), which has had both saloons reglazed when it was renovated by Hooton in 1951, carries a pair of Coronation flags above the front destination route box. The revised windows around the cab door area are of a much tidier design on this batch of the fifty EHA-registered Brush-bodied SOS FEDDs, due to the relocation of the fuel tank to a more conventional position between the wheelbase at chassis level. (A. D. Broughall)

2156, EHA 288

Standing at the last glazed cast-iron shelter in the row in St Paul's Bus Station, Walsall, is a freshly repainted 2156, (EHA 288). The bus is in the early post-war livery style with a white painted roof, unrelieved all-over red and devoid of any cream bands. The windows were rebuilt only on the lower deck but, strangely, the inset panelling over the staircase was retained, even keeping the curved bottom edge. The bus is working on the 118 to Birmingham via the Scott Arms and Perry Barr. (A. D. Packer)

2158, EHA 290

Loading up in Wolverhampton on 1 August 1938 when working on the 125 service to Birmingham is 2158, (EHA 290), the first of three EHA-registered FEDDs to be built with a full front and the radiator offset to the nearside. The three only remained in this state until 1940, as access to the engine was proving difficult on a day-to-day basis. After their conversion to half-cab, the original wider windscreen was retained. The bus has an additional slip board adding Dudley to the places the route served above the newly redesigned radiator, which had a large SOS motif in an almost AEC-type triangle. From the FHA-registered FEDDs this improved design became the standard radiator badge. (D. R. Harvey collection)

2167, EHA 299

2167, (EHA 299), was rebuilt with a concealed radiator in 1942 to act as a trial for HHA 1, the D1 prototype bus. It retained this feature until 1951, while the body's drooping streamlined upper saloon windows were never altered. However ungainly it appears, the rebuilding of 2167s was a trail-blazing modification and led to the post-war concealed radiators on nearly all post-war BMMO half-cab double-deckers. 2167 is operating on the 221 route between Bearwood and West Bromwich. (D. R. Harvey collection)

2228, FHA 210

Standing at the Malvern terminus, having just arrived on the 144 route from Birmingham via Worcester, is FHA 210. This was the last summer before the outbreak of war and this Brush-bodied SOS FEDD is only a few months old, having entered service in January 1939. The bus is in its full pomp with the final dignified pre-war livery glistening in the summer sunshine. The two triangular black glass pieces on the staircase were there to both provide a certain degree of light and modesty on the staircase. (R. Wilson)

2231, FHA 213

Travelling along Walsall Road at the junction with Tower Hill Road is 2231, (FHA 213). This Brush-bodied FEDD is working on the 119 short working to the Scott Arms terminus at the city boundary at Great Barr on 29 April 1958. This was just under a week before the route was transferred to Birmingham City Transport, whereupon it became the 51 route. This main road was for many years a single carriageway with a wide grass verge, but it was eventually made into a dual carriageway. (D. R. Harvey collection)

2234, FHA 216

It is 11 September 1949, and 2234, (FHA 216), has been parked in St Margaret's Bus Station, Leicester. The original St Margaret's had been opened alongside Burleys Way and was used extensively by Midland Red for its Leicester City services and routes towards Loughborough, Melton Mowbray, Uppingham and Oakham. 2234 has its Brush H30/26F body in its original condition, although during the following year it would be rebuilt by Hooton, giving it another useful seven years' service. The bus has inherited an earlier type of radiator from an EHA-registered vehicle. (A. D. Packer)

2257, FHA 239

The area bounded by Walsall, Wolverhampton and Wednesbury was always something of a 'closed shop' as far as Midland Red was concerned. The municipal operators of Walsall and Wolverhampton had operated both trams and trolleybuses in the area and this left Midland Red very little scope to develop new routes. One service oddity was the isolated 277 route, which ran between Willenhall and Darlaston, a distance of barely 2 miles that took only 10 minutes to complete. The route was operated by Wolverhampton Garage. On a very un-August-looking day in 1955, the driver and conductress have a brief conversation before leaving Willenhall yet again on 2257, a 1939 FEDD with a Brush H30/26F body. (D. R. Harvey collection)

2336, FHA 840

Perry Barr was an urban district in Staffordshire from 1894 until 1928, when it was absorbed into Birmingham. One of the three bus routes operated by Midland Red within the city boundary was the 188 to the Beeches Estate, just off the main Walsall Road. The 188 Beeches Estate route continued to be operated by Midland Red until handed over to Birmingham City Transport on 1 September 1957 when it was renumbered 52. 2336, (FHA 840), is at the Thornbridge Avenue–Beeches Road junction just three days before the takeover. It had been rebuilt by Aero-Engineering & Marine, (Hooton), in 1951 with all the saloon windows on both decks mounted in rubber. (D. Johnson)

2372, FHA 876
The official Brush photograph of FHA 876, taken prior to delivery in November 1939, shows all the idiosyncratic features of the FEDDs and how well Brush managed to conceal them behind a neatly proportioned facade, having a more curvaceous back with a well-rounded rear dome and pairs of matching, almost D-shaped, rear side windows in each saloon. The bottom of the front canopy was now straight – previous Brush bodies had an old-fashioned-looking concave bottom edge, while the strangely angled top step at the bottom of the doors in the porch entrance was to clear the profile of the chassis side members. In 1944 this bus received the fleet number 2372. (Brush)

2380, FHA 884
Standing opposite Midland Red's Dudley Garage in August 1952 at the terminus of all the services from Birmingham is 2380, (FHA 884). This was the penultimate SOS FEDD to enter service in November 1939 and spent most of its life operating from Oldbury Garage on routes such as the B87 service. Like many of the class, it had its Brush body rebuilt by Hooton, in this case in 1950, but only the lower saloon was reconstructed. On the other side of Birmingham Road is 1783, (BHA 381), a Metro-Cammell-bodied FEDD. In the distance is the Station Hotel and the steep climb up Castle Hill past Dudley Castle and the Zoological Gardens, located behind the trees. (R. Knibbs)

Midland Red's War-Time Double-Deckers

At the outbreak of the Second World War on 3 September 1939, the Midland Red was remarkably well placed with all the 301 SOS FEDDs and 50 SOS REDDs in service. By the end of the month these would be augmented with another fifty new vehicles that would take over the former Birmingham City Transport tram services to Smethwick, Oldbury and Dudley from BMMO's newly opened Oldbury Garage. By the end of 1939 the operational fleet of Midland Red double-deckers consisted of 401 vehicles. With the exception of the prototype D1, HHA 1, of 1944, there would be no more new double-decker chassis built at Carlyle Road for the next seven years, as the works was turned over to the manufacturing of a wide range of war materiel.

The effect on the bus industry at the outbreak of the Second World War was initially minimal but, after the retreat from Dunkirk in May 1940, the availability of new buses virtually dried up. This was because the Ministry of Supply had the authority to ensure that components, such as axles, engines, gearboxes and chassis frames that were in stock were 'frozen' as manufacturers turned over to war production.

On Loan Wartime Double-Deckers

It is often forgotten that, during the Second World War, Midland Red had to obtain on loan quite a number of double-deckers, particularly to cover the extra demand in transporting war workers to and from the various factories around the Black Country and Birmingham area.

A total of nineteen Leyland Titan TD3c dating from between 1933 and 1935 came from Bolton Corporation, the first coming on 30 March 1941. Although many were transferred away to Coventry after another severe air raid on that city on 10 April 1941, the last of these buses did not return to Lancashire until the last day of March 1942. There was one Weymann-bodied TD3c, three bodied by English Electric and two by Massey, while the remaining thirteen had bodies built locally by Bromilow & Edwards, who were based in Bolton.

In December 1941 nine London Transport ex-Thomas Tilling open-staircase AEC Regent 661 petrol-engined STs were operated until October 1944, when they returned to the capital. By coincidence, the preserved ST 922 was one of the buses hired to Midland Red. From July until December 1942 a further fourteen STs arrived from London Transport, but this time they were former General enclosed staircase buses. They were also returned in October 1944.

WH 5405

Between 1940 and 1944, BMMO suffered from a severe shortage of double-deckers, and a number of vehicles were hired to cover the increasing wartime traffic. Bolton Corporation supplied fifteen buses, one of which was their 86, (WH 5405). This was a Leyland Titan TD3c with a locally produced Bromilow & Edwards H28/23R body built in 1934. It was on loan to London Transport and is in Golder's Green when working on the 13 route in 1941. On 30 March 1941 it arrived with Midland Red. After the second air raid on Coventry, it went away to that city from 10 to 26 April 1941, after which it returned to Midland Red and stayed until the end of October the same year. (A. D. Packer)

ST 922, (GJ 2098)

A total of twenty-three petrol-engined ST class from London Transport arrived in the twelve months from December 1941 to 1942. Among the first nine was ex-Thomas Tilling ST 922, (GJ 2098), a TillingH27/25RO-bodied AEC Regent 661 dating from November 1930, whose composite body was already showing signs of sagging. It remained with Midland Red until October 1944. In early 1947, it was then converted into a mobile staff canteen, serving as fleet number 693 J until withdrawal in November 1954. Amazingly this bus was rescued by Prince J. Marshall in December 1966 and is now preserved by the London Bus Preservation Trust. It is in Trafalgar Square, having come out of Whitehall on 8 December 2005 when working on the last day of normal Routemaster operation in London on the 159 Route. (D. R. Harvey)

Midland Red's 'Unfrozen' Fleet

As the national demand for new buses grew, the next step was to use up all the reserve components to construct new vehicles. The Ministry of Supply/Ministry of War Transport, however, allowed Leyland to build 170 TD7 buses, thirty TD7s built as Merryweather turntable ladder fire engines and twenty-two Leyland Tiger TS11s. In addition AEC managed to construct another ninety-two chassis Regent 0661 model under the MoWT 'unfrozen' scheme. There were also unfrozen Bristol K5G double-deckers but only three were delivered to Midlands operators, while twenty-five 8-foot-wide buses and sixty-eight trolleybuses vehicles intended for South Africa were also allocated to UK operators.

By 1942, the BMMO was in serious need of more buses, due especially to the huge increase in the manufacturing of wartime materiel in the West Midlands operating area. The allocation of fifteen double-deck buses released by the Ministry of War Transport appears to be made on the basis of 'you have requested new vehicles and this is what we have got. Take it or leave it!' The result was the delivery of nine Leyland Titan TD7s and six AEC Regent 0661 chassis. Nine of these buses had bodies partly completed close to pre-war standard for specific customers, and six had new 'utility' bodies built to the wartime specification.

2434, GHA 788
In 1942, Midland Red was allocated some fifteen buses by the Ministry of War Transport. These were constructed from parts that were in stock at the manufacturers that had been 'frozen' by the government while companies could begin to build military vehicles. 2432, (GHA 788), the first of these buses, was a Leyland Titan TD7 with a Duple H30/26R utility body and is parked on Railway Drive, Wolverhampton, in about 1947 before the original destination box was altered to having a separate route number display. In 1951, the Duple body was rebuilt by Hooton but was withdrawn in 1954. (S. N. J. White)

2436, GHA 790

2436, (GHA 790), a Leyland Titan TD7 with an angular Duple utility body that still retains its stencil route number display, is in Navigation Street, Birmingham, where the billboard shows that Frankie Howerd was starring in *Babes in the Wood* at the Theatre Royal. It is about to work the long 196 route to Stafford via Wolverhampton. Leyland Motors had attempted, with the TD7 model, to produce a diesel-engined chassis with the quiet-running characteristics of a petrol engine. Despite the rather basic body, the chassis was quite sophisticated, but the penalty for this smooth performance was a slow gear change due to the very large flywheel. (D. R. Harvey collection)

2437, GHA 791

Parked in Cleveland Road, while a North Western Road Car Leyland-bodied Leyland Royal Tiger loads up with passengers, is 2437, (GHA 791), which was a Leyland Titan TD7 with a Duple body rebuilt to be unrecognisable by BMMO at Carlyle Road Works in 1951. Neither the 'caravan' style of rubber glazing nor the built-up nearside front wing did anything for their appearance. With their slow gear changes, these buses were much better being used on long interurban services starting in Wolverhampton, such as this 125 service, the 196 to Birmingham or the 882 to Stourbridge, where gear changes could be kept to a minimum, rather than on town routes. (D. Spencer)

2438, GHA 792

Northern Counties (NCME) bodies were always something of a rarity in the West Midlands. In 1942 Midland Red were allocated three NCME-bodied Leyland Titan TD7s by the MoWT. Parked near to Bearwood Bus Station in 1943 is the first of the trio of unfrozen Leyland Titan TD7s in an as-delivered, albeit well-worked, condition with all the accoutrements required for operating in blackout conditions. These had Northern Counties H30/26R bodies, which were metal framed and so did not conform to utility body standards. The bodies were to NCME's immediate pre-war outline, though they only had one pair of half-drop ventilators in each saloon and lacked some interior trimmings. These were the only wartime buses not to have their windows reglassed or have their bonnet and front wings rebuilt. (D. R. Harvey collection)

2432–2437 (GHA 786–791)

The first six vehicles allocated to BMMO by the Ministry of War Transport were Leyland Titan TD7s. The TD7 8.6-litre-engined model was developed with a constant-mesh four-speed gearbox and the aim of having an oil-engined vehicle that was as smooth as a petrol-engined bus. Fitted with a larger-than-normal fly-wheel, this ensured a very quiet and vibration-free idling performance but making for an extremely slow gear change. Midland Red quickly realised their limitations by using them on the longer services radiating from their home garage in Bilston Street, Wolverhampton. They were employed on long inter-urban services such as the 125 to Birmingham via Dudley and the 'New Road', the 195 to Stafford and the 882 to Stourbridge via Kingswinford.

2432–2437 (GHA 786–791), chassis numbers 307630/811/869/807–8 and 806, were fitted with Duple UH30/26R bodies. These buses were the only batch of 'unfrozen' Leyland TD7s to be fitted with Duple bodies. As was frequently the case, the delivery of these buses was somewhat protracted with 2432–2434 arriving in September 1941 and 2435–2437 coming some six months later in March 1942. Precisely for whom these buses were intended is not known, although a speculative guess suggests that the chassis were intended for Western Scottish Motor Traction.

The five-bay Duple bodies were attractively styled but had the minimum of curves. They all had upholstered seating but only a pair of half-drop windows in each saloon. The upper saloon rear emergency exit was initially unglazed and, when replaced, a strange-looking three-piece window was fitted. The Duple rear dome was made of three flat profile pieces of steel that, when welded together, looked like a lobster shell. The early wartime Duple bodywork was also easily identifiable by the wide centre pillar between the upper saloon front windows, which had top-mounted pull-in front ventilators. When these six buses were delivered, they came in an unlined red livery with two cream bands that was discontinued in 1944. The buses had just a single aperture front destination box, although immediately after the war they were fitted with a small three-number route stencil box.

The bodies were rebuilt in 1951, with 2437 being done in house by Carlyle and the other five by Hooton. All had rubber-mounted windows with four pairs of sliding ventilators in each saloon, rounded rear domes, standard destination boxes at the front, a route number blind at the rear and built-up nearside front wings that incorporated the side and headlights. All of the class were fitted with BMMO K type 8.028-litre oil engines and BMMO gearboxes in either 1952 or 1953, and were withdrawn between November 1954 and January 1955. 2433 was the longest to survive, lasting in service until 14 May 1955. Only 2434 was ever salvaged for further use, becoming a showman's lorry in Cambridgeshire.

2438–2440 (GHA 792–794)

In December 1941, Midland Red received another three Leyland Titan TD7s but this time they had Northern Counties H30/26R bodies built to semi-utility pattern. Numbered 2438–2440 (GHA 792–794), they had chassis numbers 307616–8. Again the combination of the 'unfrozen' Leyland TD7 chassis, this time coupled with highbridge Northern Counties bodies, was unusual. Coincidentally, one of the lowbridge NCME-bodied Leyland TD7s was allocated in June 1942 to the local Smethwick-based coach operator Gliderways as GHA 883, chassis number 307051, for use on the Austin Motors workmen's contract from Smethwick and Bearwood to Longbridge.

The Northern Counties bodies were metal-framed and looked similar to their standard NCME pre-war product. It was characterised by a very thick-pillared, rounded front dome, mirrored by a deep domed, rounded rear dome. At the bottom of the body there was an outwardly curved tumblehome, but generally the interior finish was distinctly on the utilitarian side, with single-skinned roofs and just a pair of half-drop opening windows in each saloon, although they did have upholstered seating. They spent their entire working lives at Bilston Street Garage, Wolverhampton, undertaking the same duties as the Duple-bodied batch.

These three Northern Counties-bodied Leyland Titan TD7 had their bodies renovated by Carlyle in 1951 but, unlike all other unfrozen and wartime 'utility' MoS-bodied buses delivered between 1942 and 1945, they were not rebuilt, and so they retained their original appearance. In 1952, 2439 and 2440 received BMMO K type engines and gearboxes, while 2438 was similarly re-engined in 1953. All three survived until the first two were withdrawn on 1 October 1955, with 2440 going on 1 December 1955.

2441–2446 (GHA 795–800)

One of the great mysteries of MoWT's allocation scheme in the Second World War was a batch of ten vehicles ordered by Coventry City Transport. Coventry had received a devastating air raid on the night of 14 November 1940, which lasted eleven hours. The city centre was destroyed and over 600 people were killed. In addition there was a loss of some forty-four trams; four buses were totally destroyed; and at least another eleven vehicles required either new bodies or major rebuilding. As a result Coventry Corporation was desperately short of buses and, after another devastating raid in April 1941, some fifty-one buses were hired.

Prior to this, in April 1940, the municipality had ordered three AEC Regent 0661s, twenty-two Daimler COA6s (all with Brush bodies) and a further twenty-five Daimler COG5s with MCCW bodies. Significantly, the three AECs would have had pre-selector gearboxes, in common with the Daimlers. However a total of sixteen Coventry-style sixty-seat bodies were constructed out of the twenty-five that were ordered. Six of the bodies were delivered to Coventry but were used in 1942 to rebody one Daimler CP6, three Daimler COA6s and two Daimler COG5/60s, all of which had their original bodies destroyed. The ten other Brush bodies were fitted to ten unfrozen AEC Regent 0661/19 chassis and, of these, only the three AEC Regents were delivered as Coventry 259–261, thus fulfilling the only part of the contract placed in 1940. These three Coventry vehicles, 259 (EVC 259–261), were delivered in January and February 1942 with chassis numbers 06617214–5 and 7197. The unfrozen chassis were fitted with the AEC A173 7.58-litre oil engines but with crash gearboxes, which were not originally specified. This left seven bodies spare and seven unfrozen AEC Regent 0661 chassis that were never part of any Coventry order!

The MoWT bureaucrats arbitrarily allocated six AEC/Brush combination buses to Midland Red to work on their intensive services in the industrialised areas of Black Country. The six Midland Red AEC Regent 0661/19s had Brush H31/28R bodies. This layout reduced the seating by one as it eliminated the rear-facing bulkhead seat in the lower saloon. Numbered 2441–2445 (GHA 795–800), with chassis numbers 06617199/98/7213/7175–76 and 7207, they were all delivered in March 1942. The Brush bodies were styled in the final peacetime Coventry design with a rather 'globular' look about them and heavily radiused bottom corners to all the front and rear saloon windows, which echoed the Brush bodies delivered on the last two batches of SOS FEDDs in 1939. The missing seventh Regent vehicle, 06617174, was delivered to Kingston-upon-Hull Corporation as their fleet number 196 (GKH 377) in April 1942.

Unlike the unfrozen Leyland TD7s, the six AEC Regents spent most of their lives operating from Harts Hill Garage in Brierley Hill, working on Stourbridge–Dudley and Stourbridge–Wolverhampton services, although their use on the 125 route between Wolverhampton and Birmingham was limited due to their small capacity engines. On these long interurban routes, the buses led fairly arduous lives and their bodies were perhaps in more need of rebuilding than the contemporary Leylands.

All six buses were renovated by Hooton in 1951 with rubber-mounted windows and a nearside front wing. The result was very ugly! In 1954, 2441/5–6 were withdrawn, while 2442–4 went the following year. After withdrawing two of the batch, 2442 and 2443 were sold by the dealer AMCC of Leyton E11 in June 1956 to Lansdowne Luxury Coaches, who were AMCC's operational division. 2443 only lasted there until September 1956, but 2442 was sold to Yeoman of Canon Pyon, Herefordshire, where it ran until 1958.

2441, GHA 795
Travelling out of Birmingham in Hagley Road West at Lightwoods Park in about 1948 is a somewhat down-at-heel 2441, (GHA 795). This Brush-bodied AEC Regent 0661 was delivered to Midland Red early in 1942 with a body built to Coventry Corporation specification, but with the seating capacity reduced by one to an H31/28R layout. 2441 is working on the 125 route to Wolverhampton on a journey timed to take 59 minutes. This bus had its body rebuilt by Hooton in 1951, but was withdrawn in 1954. (A. Porter)

2443, GHA 797
It has never been made really clear why Midland Red were allocated six AEC Regent 0661s with Brush fifty-nine seat bodies in 1942. The bodies were part of an unfulfilled order for Coventry Corporation. The AEC 7.7-litre diesel engines were already used in the DON type single-deckers of 1934 and 1935, but it was a strange allocation of buses by the Ministry of War Transport. 2441 is working on the 195 service from Birmingham to Wolverhampton in about 1943 in its as delivered livery, which included two cream bands but with added blackout markings, matt grey-painted roof and masked headlights. (R. A. Mills)

2445, GHA 799

The Dudley–Stourbridge 246 service was operated by either of the garages at the end of the route. The Hooton rebuild of the Brush bodywork on AEC Regent 0661 2445, (GHA 799), undertaken in 1951, did little to enhance the appearance of the buses in the class, especially at the front end. The intention was to modernise the half-cab area with a built-up nearside wing incorporating the head and side lights and a vertical flush cab apron. Unfortunately, although perpetuated on all the war time rebuilds, all it did was to make the bus look as though someone had just tacked on extra bits to hide the original front. 2445 stands outside Dudley Garage in 1953. (D. R. Harvey collection)

Wartime Buses

The buses allocated to the Birmingham & Midland Motor Omnibus Co. by the Ministry of War Transport were a more balanced selection than many wartime buses received by other operators. Between September 1942 and the spring of 1945, BMMO received eight Guy Arabs, later known as the Mark I, fifty Guy Arab IIs and thirty-three Daimler CWA6s, making a grand total of ninety-one wartime chassis. As far as body contracts were concerned, two were part of a pre-war streamlined styled order for Manchester Corporation, built by Metro-Cammell but completed by Weymann when their intended chassis were destroyed. All the rest were the usual composite MoS-type bodies. Forty-seven were built by Weymann, twenty by Duple, nine by Park Royal and eight by Brush. The last five wartime deliveries were metal-framed bodies built by Northern Counties. Just to add to the mix, only Weymann supplied bodies on both types of chassis, with thirty-five on Guys and five on Daimlers.

In terms of their allocation around the system, the Guy Arabs were generally operated in the Birmingham and Black Country area as well as in Leicester, while the Daimler CWA6s were exclusively used on routes radiating from Birmingham, where their 'easy-change' pre-selector gearbox Daimler could be used to good advantage.

Some operators, such as nearby Birmingham City Transport, chose to get rid of their wartime fleet of Daimlers and Guys as quickly as possible, with withdrawals starting as early as 1948 and being completed within three years. Midland Red chose the rebuilding route as, by the end of the 1940s, while chassis were still sound, many of these wartime bodies were in a bad way with rotting pillars, body's moving and half-drop ventilators getting stuck at an angle because the window frames were no longer square. Steel parts such as wheel arches had often corroded, while rear platforms were sagging. BMMO were still intent on building their own buses but, when the programme began in 1949, they had only received one of the AD2 class of post-war AEC Regent II o661/20s and seventy of the 100 Brush-bodied BMMO D5s. So Midland Red were short of new double-decker buses at the end of the 1940s and most of the Brush pre-war SOS FEDDs were also in dire need of a rebuild, beginning in 1948 and completed by 1951. In 1950 for example, some seventy-four pre-war double-deckers and another forty-two wartime buses were away at some stage for rebuilding. In retrospect one has to wonder about the economic viability of undertaking such a large rebuilding project, one that only lengthened the life of the wartime vehicles by a maximum of six or seven years. Perhaps another fifty new double-decker buses bought from an outside manufacturer might have been better, but new chassis availability was at a premium. Withdrawals of the wartime fleet, with one exception, took place between 1955 and 1957, being replaced by new BMMO D7s.

The First Guys Arrive

From September 1942 until November 1943, all the eighteen buses received by Midland Red that were allocated by the Ministry of War Transport were Guy Arabs. These rugged, no-nonsense buses were a bit underpowered, with only a 7.0-litre Gardner engine, and were hard work for their drivers, who had to contend with a back-to-front crash gearbox that had the usual H configuration but with first gear where normally fourth gear was located and vice versa with fourth gear on the top left position. Nevertheless, they were reliable, robust and straightforward to maintain.

2452–2457 (GHA 886–891)

The first buses allocated by the MoWT to Midland Red were six wartime Guy Arabs. A total of 500 of this first type were constructed and could be distinguished by having short, straight front wings. Coincidentally, neighbouring Birmingham City Transport's first five 'utility' double-deckers were of the same chassis and body combination. The five Midland Red buses, 2452–2457 (GHA 886-891), were fitted with a standard MoS-designed wartime body built by Weymann, with the normal H30/26R layout. They had the usual pull-in front window ventilators but had, unusually, a pair of sliding saloon ventilators as well as fully upholstered seating. Buses had a standard single wartime destination box with a separate three-track stencil route number box.

The first three buses, 2452–2454, entered service on 1 September 1942, while November saw the rest arrive. The first three of these Guy Arab Is were among the first twenty-five chassis of this type to be constructed and were also the second, third and fourth wartime bodies built by Weymann. From 1944 these five Arabs transferred to Sandacre Street Garage, Leicester, from Sutton Coldfield Garage.

All six buses were renovated by Brush with 2452–53/55 and 2457 being rebuilt in 1950, while 2454 and 2456 were reconstructed in 1951. The rebuilding included all the windows being remounted in rubber glazing with sliding ventilators in the saloons. The ventilators used by Brush were quite distinctive, having their own discrete glazing from the fixed pane beneath them. The rear dome was reconstructed with a more rounded roof line, but it retained the upper saloon single-skinned ceiling. The front profile survived the rebuilding, keeping the pull-in front ventilators in the front upper saloon windows. Yet the destination boxes on the front had a three-track nearside route number display. The interiors were re-upholstered in brown and rust moquette.

2453 was withdrawn on 5 January 1955, another three in 1956 and then 2457 on 1 February 1957, which became the final wartime bus to remain in service. 2453 eventually finished its career with a showman, leaving only 2456 to re-enter service as a bus, in this case with Warner of Tewkesbury.

2497–2498 (GHA 921–922)

On 23 February 1943, 2497–2498 (GHA 921–922) entered service with Midland Red. These were another pair of Guy Arabs with the usual 7.0-litre Gardner 5LW engine.

Like the previous five Arabs, they had Weymann MoWT style fifty-six-seater bodies. These buses were very camera shy in their original state but, unlike the earlier Weymann bodies, they had a pair of half-drop windows in each saloon. Wooden slatted seats appeared for the first time in the fleet but were replaced with upholstered seating between November 1945 and October 1947. Both buses had their bodies rebuilt by Brush, with 2497 being renovated in 1950 and 2498 in 1951, making them look identical in this form as 2452–2457. 2498 was withdrawn on 11 October 1955, while 2497 went on 1 November the following year, both being subsequently broken up.

2499–2500 (GHA 923–924)

Although mounted on the wartime Guy Arab chassis, these two bodies were of the streamlined pre-war type intended for Manchester Corporation. They were constructed on Metro-Cammell frames for Daimler COG5 chassis but, after Radford Works in Coventry was destroyed, the remaining fifteen body frames were re-directed by the MoWT to be finished by Weymann at Addlestone, with less luxuriant interiors than intended. Further examples of this combination were delivered to Sheffield Corporation, who had five, while Coventry, Newport and Midland General each received a pair.

The two buses were numbered 2499 and 2500 (GHA 923 and 924). Their H30/26R metal-framed bodies were quite distinctive, with curved and drooping upper saloon front windows, while the rear side saloon windows on each deck were also curved downwards. The pair had just a hint of austerity about them, with only two pairs of half-drop windows in the upper saloon and a single pair in the lower saloon. They entered service on 23 February 1943 on the same day as 2497–2498 and spent their entire lives allocated to Sutton Garage.

In 1951 the bodies were renovated by Hooton, who replaced the original route and destination boxes with the standard large post-war version, and as per usual Midland Red's own hideously built-up cab apron front and nearside front wing. Both were withdrawn on New Year's Day 1956, having led fairly uneventful lives after the interesting start to their careers.

2501–2508 (GHA 925–932)

The next batch of eight buses was also bodied by Weymann with standard MoS-type bodywork. The difference was that these vehicles were the Guy Arab II model. This chassis differed from the original wartime Arab by having the radiator extended in front of the cab apron in order to accommodate, where necessary, the 7½-inch-longer Gardner 6LW 8.4-litre engine. Additionally, the leading edge of the front wings was curved upwards to be level with the vertical face of the radiator. Amendments to the Construction and Use Regulations allowed the Arab II chassis to be extended by 9 inches to 26 feet 9 inches to accommodate the 6LW engines. All of the Midland Red Guy Arab IIs were fitted with the shorter Gardner 5LW engine with the new radiused front wings.

In September 1943, Midland Red received 2501 (GHA 925), the next four arriving in October 1943, while 2506–2508 entered service in November, all going to Sutton Coldfield Garage. Like the previous Arabs, they had Weymann MoS-style fifty-six-seater bodies with a pair of half-drop windows in each saloon and were fitted with wooden slatted seats. Upholstered units replaced these in the reseating programme between November 1945 and October 1947. Most of this batch of Guy Arab IIs was transferred to Sandacre Street Garage, Leicester.

All eight buses were rebuilt by Brush in 1951, but the radiator was put back into the original Arab position level, flush with the front of the cab. In this form it was very difficult to tell apart the two Arab models. The distinctive saloon glazing, with the windows and ventilators being mounted in separate rubber mountings, was continued again.

2504 was an early accident victim, and was dismantled in November 1953. The rest were gradually taken out of service, with the last to go being 2507, which lasted until 31 March 1956. 2454, 2505, 2507 and 2508 were cut down and used by showmen.

The Arrival of Daimler CWA6s

The next buses supplied to Midland Red were some thirty-three Daimler CWA6s. The CWA6 model was a direct successor to Coventry's unique pre-war COA6s, with a Wilson pre-selector gearbox. They had an AEC A173 7.58-litre engine but it was bolted directly to the frame, which often led to vibration at the top end of the rev range. However, the AEC engine was free-revving and had a quite lively performance, being able to accelerate quite quickly with very fast gear changes using the pre-selector gearbox. This suited the model to intensive urban work with the Midland Red examples spending their entire lives in the Birmingham area, all being garaged at Digbeth from new until 1951. In 1951 twenty-eight of the buses were part of the initial allocation to Sheepcote Street when it opened that year. The bodywork was supplied by three body builders.

2509–2513 (GHA 933–937)

The first batch of pre-selector gearboxed Daimler CWA6s was bodied by Weymann. These were virtually identical to the Weymann bodies fitted to the earlier Guy Arabs and were also fitted with wooden slatted seats. As usual, they were delivered in the normal red livery with two cream bands, before they were painted all-over red during their first renovation between 1945 and 1947, when their wooden slatted seats were also replaced. The five buses were delivered over a period of four months. 2509 entered service in September 1943, with 2512–2513 coming in December 1943. One of the buses, 2511, was fitted with a Daimler CD6 engine between 1945 until 1952, even surviving its body rebuild in 1950, before being re-engined in 1952 with an AEC 7.58-litre engine.

The main body reconstruction of 2509–2513 took place in 1950. This was by Willowbrook of Loughborough, producing a rebuild that was subtly different from those reconstructed by Brush. The saloon windows were mounted in rubber but only the bottom corners had a radius. As with the Guys, the nearside front wing was built up, as was the apron beneath the cab, which matched the angle of the slightly sloping radiator. In addition, the offside side light was placed just below the windscreen, while all five were fitted with post-war front destination boxes.

These Daimlers were all withdrawn in 1956, with the exception of 2511, which went during the previous year. Three of the buses served other operators, with 2509 going to Northern Roadways of Glasgow; 2510 going to Yuille of Larkhall; 2511 operating briefly between December 1955 and May 1956 for Lansdowne Luxury Coaches, before being sold to Trimdon Motor Services in County Durham; and 2512 working in the Leeds area for Samuel Ledgard.

2514–2522 (GHA 938–946)

The next Daimler CWA6s were nine vehicles fitted with Duple bodies, delivered at the very end of 1943. Although looking fairly flimsy, the MoS regulation bodies coming out of their Hendon factory were often some of the best composite wartime bodies, having extra rigidity with the lower saloon waist rail being deeper than many other 'utility' bodies The Duple body could be easily distinguished by having a three-piece 'lobster'-shaped rear dome and an angled corner to the rear of the driver's door. The buses had just a pair of opening half-drop windows in each saloon and wooden-slatted seats.

After the customary replacement of the wooden seats, the buses remained in their original condition until 1950, when 2515–2518 and 2520–2522 were rebuilt by Willowbrook. 2514 and 2519 were reconstructed in 1951. Three of these vehicles, 2514, 2516 and 2518, were withdrawn in 1955, while the last three, 2515, 2517 and 2520, survived until 1 October 1956. The second-hand market must have favoured these Duple bodies rebuilds for Midland Red, as seven of the nine were sold for further use.

2530–2540 (GHA 965–975)

Another eleven Duple-bodied Daimler CWA6s entered service between February and May 1944. They were 2530–2540 (GHA 965–975) and came with the usual red livery with two cream bands and a matt grey painted roof and the usual black painted radiators. The Duple bodies were the same as the previous 2514–2522 class of vehicles. Both batches had the less common type of Duple body with the bottom of the driver's cab door being level with the lower saloon windows.

All eleven buses were re-seated with upholstered seats between 1945 and 1947, and subsequently went to Willowbrook for rebuilding, seven being dealt with in 1950 and the other four being completed in 1951. One major difference between the Willowbrook rebuilds and those done by Brush was that in the lower saloon there were only four sliding ventilators on each side rather than five. As was normal, the extension on the lives of these rebuilt buses was not very long, with 2532, 2537 and 2539 being withdrawn in 1955 and the balance of eight going during the following year. Eight of these buses were sold for further PSV use.

1944: the D1

The Ministry of Supply gave Midland Red permission to build a double-decker bus as a prototype for their post-war vehicles. The new general manager, Mr Donald Sinclair, was firmly against the continuation of the FEDD front entrance concept. The resulting development began in 1944 and, by late 1945, the new bus 2541 (HHA 1) entered service as the 1944 REDD. The chassis of the bus, given the penultimate pre-war series chassis number 2893, had its roots in the 1939 FEDD with the same 8.028-litre oil engine but with improved flexible engine mountings. The Germany ZF gearbox was impossible to obtain, but a BMMO version of this type of four-speed constant mesh gearbox was developed. The transmission was then taken to an underslung worm-driven back axle. The wheelbase of the new chassis was 16-foot 3-inch, while the brakes were modified, having hydraulically powered servo-assistance, thus making the driver's job far easier. It was apparently the first oil-engined double-decker chassis in the UK to have this method of braking using a hydraulic pump.

The experimental concealed radiator design for EHA 299 re-emerged on 2541 but the front was spoilt by the narrow FEDD-style front tyres. The four-bay metal-framed body was built by Weymann, which had that company's body number M2667 and had an H30/26R seating layout. The saloon windows were fitted into radiused window pans and each saloon had four sliding ventilators. The heavily curved front upper saloon windows gave the bus a somewhat worried look. For the first time on a Midland Red double-decker, two front destination boxes on the off side and a triple-track number blind replaced stencil route numbers. This transformed the Midland Red buses at a stroke from having probably the least readable number boxes in the country to having possibly the clearest! There were also two narrow rear destination boxes, one for the final destination and a smaller route number box.

The bus was delivered with a flat two-piece windscreen with a somewhat 'anxious-looking' top profile that was modified before it entered service with a recessed top half developed to prevent reflections from the lower saloon at night. This obsession with reflections onto the windscreen seems to be a particular West Midlands fixation as Birmingham City Transport 'New Look front' buses also had this feature. Above the front of the canopy was a long, horizontal mesh-covered duct, which was used to supply air for the saloon heaters. In 1949 the bus was fitted at Carlyle Road Works with an enclosed rear platform including a two-piece, four-windowed concertina door and a centrally mounted emergency exit on the rear wall of the platform. This arrangement was used on the Brush-bodied BMMO D5B buses with 2541 used as the prototype. In this form the bus weighed 7 tons 13 cwt 1qtrs, some 4 hundredweight more than in its original open platform state. At the same time that the platform was being enclosed, the windscreen was unaccountably returned to the original flat two-piece arrangement.

Built in 1945, the D1 was one of the first buses with concealed radiator and bonnet assemblies in Britain. The D1 had a well-finished, lightweight Weymann four-bay body, incorporating smoothly curved lines. 2541 was always allocated to Bearwood Garage, where it was used on the 125 route from Birmingham to Wolverhampton. Later it operated on the 220 and 221 routes from West Bromwich to Bearwood Bus Station, where it always seemed to be parked. The bus remained in service until 1961 when it was withdrawn.

2542–2549 (GHA 992–999)

These eight buses were the last Daimler CWA6s to be allocated by the MoWT to Midland Red and were the only wartime buses delivered with Brush bodywork. 2542 and 2543 entered service in December 1944, leaving the remaining six vehicles to enter service between January and February 1945. Brush bodywork had reappeared in highbridge form on the Daimler CWA6 chassis in October 1944 and these Midland Red Daimler CWA6s entered service at the same time as the Brush-bodied examples supplied as 120–124 to nearby West Bromwich Corporation.

The Brush bodies only had one pair of half-drop ventilators in each saloon and retained the shell backed rear dome with a distinctive rectangular single pane emergency window. These bodies were easily identifiable by the slightly raised lip and apron underneath the windscreen and a deep waist rail below the lower saloon windows. All eight buses were delivered with the wooden slatted seats replaced with the upholstered variety between November 1945 and October 1947.

One of the class, 2546, was the trial Daimler CWA6 rebuild. This was undertaken at Carlyle Road Central Works in 1949. On both sides of the lower saloon, the front and rear windows had rounded upper and lower corners, giving them a slightly D-shaped look. The sliding ventilators had curved tops that were matched by a similarly shaped curved profile. The sloping radiator and cab apron were moved forward from the original position and the nearside wing assembly was rebuilt to the usual Midland Red design. The bus was withdrawn on 1 July 1955. The remainder of the class were rebuilt by Willowbrook, with 2542–2544 and 2547 being treated in 1950, while the remaining three were rebuilt in 1951. 2542, 2544–2545 and 2547 were taken out of service in 1955, and 2543, 2548 and 2549 went the following year. Five of these buses were to see further PSV service.

Back to Guy Arabs; 2550–2569 (HHA 2–21); 2573–2578 (HHA 25–30)

Numerically, the next buses delivered to Midland Red were two batches of Guy Arab IIs with the usual Gardner 5LW engine. They were allocated by the MoS with Weymann H30/26R bodies and totalled twenty-six vehicles. When new these buses were delivered in lined-out red with two cream bands and a grey roof with the usual masked headlights and white painted life rails and mudguard edges. They had wooden slatted seats, which were replaced between late 1945 and the autumn of 1947. The bodies were the same as the previous Weymann products delivered on the Daimler CWA6s 2512–2513.

These buses took over eight months to be delivered! 2550–2552 entered service in March 1944. By July 1944 deliveries had reached 2561. Again there was a pause in deliveries, with 2564–2569 arriving in October. The first of the next batch, 2573, whose chassis number of FD 27071 was the next one after 2568, also entered service in October 1944 with 2575 to 2578 arrived in November 1944; these were the final bodies delivered from the Addlestone bodybuilder.

2578 was chosen as the prototype Carlyle body rebuild on a Guy Arab II chassis and was the first rebuild to be attempted on any of the buses delivered to the company between 1942 and 1945. This trial served as an economic experiment to see if it was viable to undertake the rebuilding of the entire wartime double-deck bus fleet. 2578 was unique among all the wartime bus rebuild by only having four pairs of sliding ventilators in the upper saloon, but in all other aspects was the same as the prototype Daimler CWA6 Carlyle rebuild 2546, also completed in 1949. All the rest of these two batches of Weymann-bodied Guy Arab IIs were rebuilt in the usual style by Brush in 1950 and 1951. The withdrawal of the vehicles took three years to complete. 2551 and 2561 went in 1954, another ten went in 1955, and eleven in 1956. This left 2557 and the prototype Carlyle rebuild 2578 to be taken out of service on 1 January 1957, while 2559 went exactly a month later as one of the last pair wartime buses to be withdrawn by Midland Red.

Three of these buses were sold for further PSV use, notably 2574, which was sold to Warner of Tewkesbury, who fitted it with platform doors. This bus was eventually purchased for preservation by the late Colin Hawketts, who rebuilt the Weymann body back to its original 'utility' form. Four of the rest, 2554, 2566, 2568 and 2573, were not quite as fortunate as they were cut down for use as showmen's vehicles.

2570–2572 (HHA 22–24); 2580–2585 (HHA 57-62)

It was surprising that just nine wartime Park Royal bodies were delivered to Midland Red, as this was most common body to be delivered to West Midlands operators with Birmingham, Coventry, Walsall and Wolverhampton Corporations all getting large numbers. Of this first batch of 7.0-litre Gardner 5LW-engined Guy Arab IIs, three were delivered to BMMO as 2570–2572 (HHA 22–24), with the first two arriving in March 1944 and the last vehicle coming in the following month. The second batch were another six, numbered 2580–2585 (HHA 57–62). 2584 was delivered to Midland Red in October 1944 while the first four came in November and 2585 arrived in December 1944.

The Park Royal wartime MoS body was arguably the best looking of all the wartime bodies, particularly around the cab area, where all the tops of windows and canopies were at the same level; the sloping bottom edge of the windscreen had below it just a hint of an angled ledge to form the top of the cab apron. Both batches of these Park Royal-bodied buses had a fairly rigid interpretation of the wartime MoWT design with upper saloon front opening ventilators and just a pair of half-drop windows in each saloon. The rear dome was square but neatly proportioned. 2580–2585 were the last buses delivered with wooden slatted seats. Re-seating followed the normal early post-war pattern, much to the relief of the passengers in the Birmingham area where they were in operation.

Many Park Royal bodies were not necessarily the most robust, due in part to the poor quality wood used in the framework and also to all of the buses being rebuilt by

Brush, which totally disfigured the original Park Royal bodywork. In 1950 2571, 2580 and 2581 were rebuilt, while 2570, 2572 and 2582–2585 were dealt with during 1951. This extended their lives with Midland Red for about five years, with 2581 being taken out of use early on 15 December 1954, while the last one, 2571, was withdrawn on 1 November 1956. These examples were the shortest lived of all Midland Red's wartime buses. Despite their reconstruction, only 2585 ran again as a PSV, this time with Warner of Tewkesbury; 2581, ironically the first withdrawal, finished as a showman's lorry.

2586–2590 (HHA 81–85)

At the very end of wartime deliveries Midland Red were allocated five Guy Arab IIs but this time with metal-framed Northern Counties H30/26R bodies, which beneath the surface were very similar to the unfrozen trio of Leyland Titan TD7s. These buses were delivered in red with two bands of cream and with brown roofs in March 1945.

Delivered to Leicester's Sandacre Street Garage in March 1945, these five buses spent their entire lives there. The buses could be easily identified by their deep roof line and inset saloon windows mounted in window pans. They still had a lobster-shaped four-piece angular rear dome and had only two pairs of half-drop windows in the upper saloon but, for the first time since the unfrozen double-deckers of 1942, these buses came with the luxury of upholstered seats.

All five were rebuilt by Hooton in 1951 but, as with the metal-framed Weymann-bodied Guy Arab Is 2499 and 2500, all that was altered was a set of post-war destination blinds and the ugly built-up nearside wing and cab apron. Three of the buses, 2586, 2588 and 2590, were taken out of service during 1956 with 2587 surviving until New Year's Day 1957. Only 2589 (HHA 89) went on to be operated as a PSV, having been sold to Gosport & Fareham where it ran until 1963 before being re-engined with an air-cooled Deutz engine and fitted with a full-fronted Reading H30/26R body and re-entering service during the following year. It survived to be taken over by Hants & Dorset on 1 January 1970, after which it was quickly withdrawn.

2452, GHA 886

Overleaf above: Parked on the waste ground opposite St Margaret's Bus Station off Abbey Street in Leicester, used by the company for parking buses out of the way until their next tour of duty, is the rebuilt 2452, (GHA 886). This Guy Arab I had the usual Gardner 5LW 7.0-litre engine that developed 85 hp at 1,700 rpm. It was fitted with one of the first Weymann MoS-style bodies and was delivered to Midland Red in September 1942. It had its body rebuilt by Brush in 1950 and retained its H30/26R layout. The rebuilding gave 2452 an extra six years in service. (S. N. J. White)

2454, GHA 888

Overleaf below: The rugged lines of the un-rebuilt Weymann UH30/26R bodywork probably looked better than in its rebuilt state. 2454, (GHA 888), a Guy Arab I was delivered in September 1942 and, unusually, came with upholstered seats. The first 500 Arabs had its radiator mounted almost flush with the front apron and had straight wings. It is parked in Leicester on 25 June 1950 and the following year it was rebuilt by Brush surviving until 1956. Behind it is 1924, (CHA 548), a 1936 SOS SON with an English Electric B39F body. (A. D. Packer)

2497, GHA 921

2497, (GHA 921), has just arrived in Leicester, having worked into the city from Uppingham via Thurmaston along the A47 on the 617 route. This Guy Arab I was delivered to Midland Red as one of a pair delivered in February 1943 and fitted with a Weymann UH30/26R body. It was recently rebuilt by Brush in 1950; their rebuilds for Midland Red could be identified by the saloon ventilators having rounded ends and being separate from the main windows. (S. N. J. White)

2500, GHA924

2499 and 2500 were two more Guy Arab Is but were fitted with semi-streamlined Weymann metal-framed H30/26R bodywork. These bodies had been intended for Daimler COG5s for Manchester Corporation but became available after their chassis were destroyed in the air raid on Coventry on 14 November 1940, when the Radford works was bombed. Midland Red received two bodies, which were fitted to Guy Arab chassis, and the buses entered service in 1943. 2500, (GHA 924), the second of the pair is in High Street, Birmingham, outside the Co-operative department store and is about to work on the busy 118 route to Walsall via Six Ways, Aston. (R. A. Mills)

2500, GHA924

2500, (GHA924), spent its operational life at Upper Holland Street Garage in Sutton Coldfield and is leaving The Parade shopping centre in the centre of the town, having been rebuilt by Hooton. It is working on the 107 service to Birmingham via New Oscott and Perry Barr, which was timed to take 37 minutes. The two Guys with 'Manchester'-style Metro-Cammell bodies were, externally at least, a complete contrast to the usual austerity bodies. These bodies were metal-framed and so the rebuilding in 1951 was confined to the standard post-war destination boxes and built-up nearside front wing and cab apron. (J. Wyndham)

2504, GHA 928

The Arab II was distinguishable from its immediate predecessor by having an extended bonnet and curved front mudguards in order to line up with the radiator. This was done in order that these buses could accept the longer Gardner 6LW 8.4-litre engine, though all of the examples operated by Midland Red had the more common, smaller Gardner 5LW engine. 2504, (GHA 928), another Weymann UH30/26R-bodied Guy Arab II, has recently arrived at St Margaret's Bus Station, having arrived in Leicester on the profitable 625 service from Loughborough and Rothley. It is parked off Abbey Street on 25 June 1950. (A. D. Packer)

2508, GHA 932
Recently returned from Brush Coachworks after its body reconstruction in 1951 is 2508, (GHA 932), and it looks very smart with its lined out livery. The rebuilt bodywork's upper saloon front corners were much squarer than other coachbuilders' rebuilds. This Guy Arab II had a Weymann UH30/26R and was delivered in November 1943. It is parked in High Street, Birmingham, and is about to leave on the 107 service to Sutton Coldfield via New Oscott. Despite the cost of this reconstruction, 2508 was withdrawn in 1955. (P. Yeomans)

2509, GHA 933
The first of the wartime Daimler CWA6s to be delivered to Midland Red arrived in September 1943 with Weymann UH30/26R bodywork, which somehow looked more subtle, despite being virtually the same, than when it was mounted on the Guy Arab chassis. 2509, (GHA 933), is parked in High Street in Birmingham on 31 March 1946. It has arrived in the city centre having worked on the 168 service and is about to make the return journey back to Coleshill. Although the bus is in its original cream-banded lined-out livery, it is beginning to look in need of a repaint. (R. Wilson)

2512, GHA 936

Travelling along Digbeth in July 1954 is Daimler CWA6 2512, (GHA 936). By this time its Weymann wartime body had been subjected to the Midland Red rebuilding treatment by Willowbrook in 1950, which hardly enhanced the vehicle's appearance. It is parked opposite Digbeth Garage on the corner of Rea Street, awaiting a change of crew before proceeding to Coventry on the 159 service. On the former bus parking lot adjacent to the garage work has recently begun on the block of shops and flats, which will form a part of the Spencer House office complex, yet to be started. (R. Knibbs)

2516, GHA 940

Climbing up the steep hill in Washwood Road and passing the BCT tram depot in about 1948 is 2516, (GHA 940). This Daimler CWA6 had a Duple UH30/26R body and was delivered to Midland Red in November 1943. It is being used on the 161 service from Coleshill by way of Castle Bromwich and the Fox & Goose tram terminus. The bus has by now lost its original red with two cream bands livery although the BMMO garter remains on the front cab apron. (A. Yates)

2530, GHA 965

Delivered in January 1944, three-month-old Duple-bodied Daimler CWA6, in the attractive wartime livery and full blackout markings, comes out of Camp Hill and negotiates the traffic island at the top of Sandy Lane when working out of the city on a route using Stratford Road. The 'lobster tail' shape of the rear dome was a characteristic of wartime Duple double-deck bodywork, which, despite its frail appearance, was surprisingly strong due to extra longitudinal body rails below the saloon windows, giving body both strength and rigidity. (Birmingham CRL)

2536, GHA 971

2536, (GHA 971), a rebuilt Daimler CWA6, is working on the 169 short working service in Castle Bromwich and is on its way into Birmingham from Bacons End in 1953. It is picking up passengers; it can only be hoped that the running man eventually caught the bus. It was delivered to Midland Red in February 1944, becoming one of the last buses to arrive without a fleet number, this being allocated two months later. This Duple-bodied bus was rebuilt by Willowbrook in 1950 and withdrawn in July 1956. (A. Yates)

2541, HHA 1

Two photographs of 2541, (HHA 1), the Weymann-bodied SOS 1944 REDD, when new in 1945, shows the nearside and offside of this wartime prototype. It is parked at the Beeches Estate terminus of the 188 route and still has the early location of the nearside fleet number positioned on the bonnet. The bus, reclassified BMMO D1 in 1945, has its original open rear platform and looks as if it has been worked hard, judging by the mud spray on both flanks. (D. R. Harvey collection)

2541, HHA1

Overtaking a parked Ford Anglia 100E two-door saloon in St Mary's Road, Bearwood, is 2541, (HHA 1), the D1 prototype with its unique Weymann H30/26R body. The bus is working from Bearwood on the 221 service to Dartmouth Square, West Bromwich via Warley. The bus is in its final state being fitted with an enclosed platform with electric doors in 1949 and acting as a trial for the later BMMO D5Bs. (A. D. Broughall)

2541, HHA1

In later years, whenever one passed through Bearwood 2541, (HHA 1), always seemed to be there. The Weymann-bodied BMMO D1 often frequented the bus station itself and was regularly turned out on the 220 service to Dartmouth Square in West Bromwich. In 1961, in company with the almost-new BMMO D9, 4859, (859 KHA), HHA 1 is parked in Bearwood Bus Station. Rebuilt in 1949 with an enclosed rear platform, this required the neat solution of putting the emergency door on the back of the bus. The result acted as a prototype for the enclosed platforms fitted to the Brush-bodied BMMO D5Bs. (P. Tizard)

2542, GHA 992

The Midland Red bus services operating from St Paul's Bus Station in Walsall used the bottom stance that was on the other side from where the Corporation trolleybuses loaded up. Waiting at the 118 stop is 2542, (GHA 992), the first of the Brush-bodied Daimler CWA6s delivered in December 1944. By this time, the bodywork had been rebuilt by Willowbrook in 1950. Parked behind it is a Metro-Cammell-bodied SOS FEDD, while parked in front of the Walsall Transport offices is a pre-war Corporation Dennis Lancet II with a Park Royal body. (M. C. Dare)

2543, GHA 993

Parked behind a 1935 Hillman Minx outside the Co-op in High Street, Birmingham, is 2543, (GHA 993). This Daimler CWA6 had a Brush UH30/26R body and was just over five years old in this un-rebuilt state having entering service in December 1944. It is being used on the 161 route to Water Orton and Coleshill, though the stencil plate has fallen backwards, making it difficult to read. The Midland Red wartime Daimlers were used extensively in the Birmingham area, where their pre-selector gearboxes made driving in heavy traffic much easier. Behind it is 3247, JHA 847, a 1948-built Metro-Cammell-bodied BMMO S8. (Birmingham CRL)

2555, HHA7

Standing in St Margaret's Bus Station in Leicester is Weymann-bodied Guy Arab II 2555, (HHA7). Delivered in April 1944, 2555 was, like most of the Midland Red fleet of Guys, rebuilt by Brush in 1950. Curiously, after their rebuilding, the wartime buses retained the white-covered platform stanchions, which were a remnant of the wartime blackout regulations. It was taken out of service in July 1956 when just over twelve years old, leaving one to wonder if their reconstruction was an economically viable option. (E. Surfleet)

2559, HHA 11

2559, (HHA 11), is in its 'as delivered' livery with a matt-grey roof, two cream livery bands, lower saloon lining out and all the paraphernalia associated with the wartime blackout regulations. Its conductor stands on the nearside dumb iron as she speaks to the driver sitting in his cab while they wait in High Street, Birmingham, when about to work on the 107 service to Sutton Coldfield via New Oscott. This Guy Arab II had a Weymann UH30/26R body and entered service in July 1944; it was one of forty-five of this type to be allocated to Sutton Garage. (C. Klapper)

2572, HHA 24

On 27 November 1953 2572, (HHA 24), is parked on the forecourt of Sutton Coldfield Garage in Upper Holland Street. This bus was one of three Park Royal-bodied Guy Arab IIs delivered to Midland Red in the spring of 1944. It was rebuilt in 1951 by Brush and ran in this condition until June 1956. The garage was opened on 26 August 1934 and, for several years, was only occupied by single-deckers as the town council would not allow double-deckers to operate into the town. (D. R. Harvey collection)

2582, HHA 59

As the Birmingham City Transport 'New Look fronted' Daimler CVD6 has lost its decorative
wheel discs, it would have been about 1954 when 2582, (HHA 59), stood at its High Street
terminus. This Park Royal-bodied Guy Arab II dated from early 1945 and was among the last
buses delivered to Midland Red with wooden slatted seats. It was rebuilt by Brush in 1951.
It is working on the 118 route to Walsall but has the less common Perry Barr intermediate
destination display. (D. R. Harvey collection)

2587, HHA 82

Above: The metal-framed Northern Counties bodywork on the last five wartime Guys barely needed rebuilding but, unlike the composite bodywork on the other Midland Red Guys, these were renovated, along with the Manchester-style bodies on 2499–2500, by Aero & Engineering (Merseyside) Ltd, better known as 'Hooton'. 2589, (HHA 84), stands opposite St Margaret Bus Station after it had been to Hooton in 1951 and received the unfortunately styled front wing and bonnet assembly. It was withdrawn in 1956. (P. Yeomans)

2573, HHA 25

Opposite above: The first of six Weymann-bodied Guy Arab IIs, 2573, (HHA 25), entered service in October 1944. The bus is very low on its rear springs because of its full load as it reaches the top of Station Street at the junction with Worcester Street. Behind the bus is the LMS Parcels Office serving New Street Station. It is working on the 198 route to Tamworth. This was several years before the bus would be rebuilt by Brush in 1951. (S. N. J. White)

1948–1952: Early Post-War Double-Deckers

The introduction of new double-deckers built by the company, developed from the D1 prototype 2541 (HHA 1), was delayed by the company concentrating on the new S type underfloor-engined single-deckers between 1946 and 1950. The result was that the first 'home-built' double-deck Carlyle product did not enter service until 1949. Midland Red's urgent need for new buses meant that they had to purchase chassis built by other manufacturers.

When the war ended, Britain was economically crippled by its expenses during it. The new Attlee Labour government developed the policy of 'export or bust' while at the same time nationalising power supplies, transport, ports haulage and introducing the National Health Service and restructuring the education system. And, out of these economic constraints, Midland Red's first post-war underfloor-engined S6 single-decker emerged in October 1946! BMMO began a programme of bus production that would, in the space of five years, see the demise of two-thirds of the pre-war bus fleet and put 500 homemade single-deckers and 200 double-deckers on the road. Unfortunately it was in this last category that Midland Red really had its production shortfall. Production of the Carlyle-built D5 type double-decker had to be delayed and the first examples were not going to be ready until around 1949.

The AD2s

As a result of this delay, the company looked to an outside chassis manufacturer for their first post-war double-deckers. The order was placed in 1945/46 for 100 AEC Regent II 0661/20s. This was the first time that Midland Red had bought double-deckers from another manufacturer in peacetime. The AD2 (AEC Double-deck) types took an inordinately long time to enter service. These 26-foot-long by 7-foot-6-inch-wide buses had the AEC 7.58-litre engine coupled to a four-speed crash gearbox, which, with judicious double-declutching, made for a very civilised, if somewhat sedate ride. These early post-war buses sounded similar to the unfrozen 1942 AEC Regents, numbered 2441–2446.

The order for metal-framed four-bay construction bodies was split between Brush and Metro-Cammell with identical seating capacities of H30/26R. These buses were partially delayed by Midland Red's requirement that they be fitted with the concealed radiator assembly, which had been finalised on 2541 (HHA 1). The first fifty were bodied by Brush and were numbered 3100–49 (JHA 1–50). The Brush bodies could be easily distinguished from the later MCCW-bodied examples with sliding ventilators in only the first and third bays of each saloon, making just four opening windows on each deck. This compared with a continuous line of four sliding opening windows on each side of each saloon on the Metro-Cammell bodied AD2s, which did give a more 'complete' appearance. The second major identifying feature on the Brush bodies was that the Brush bodies were built in separate lower and upper saloons, with a heavy moulding at the upper saloon floor level that also acted as a continuous gutter around the bus. The Metro-Cammell examples were built as one unit and did not have the external guttering. The AD2s were delivered with a pair of single-line rear destination boxes mounted side-by-side with a long nearside destination box and a small separate route number box, although 3101 (JHA 2), at least, was delivered with a single triple indicator route number box of the style first fitted to the S9 single-deckers. The Metro-Cammell bodies could be distinguished from the Brush examples by having three drainage ducts at cant-rail height over the lower saloon windows, while the front upper saloon windows were slightly more recessed with a heavier moulding between the front dome and the window tops. All the buses came in all-over red without any cream relief, but were lined out in yellow and had black wings. The concealed radiator had nineteen horizontal slats arranged in two vertical columns and surmounted by the chrome legend 'BMMO'. There was no indication on the bonnet that they were manufactured by AEC. The bodies on both batches were internally well appointed. The lower saloon moquette was an attractive orange, fawn and brown with white painted ceilings and red-painted side panels, staircase and open back platform.

The first Brush-bodied AD2 3100, (JHA 1) entered service on 25 March 1948, some six weeks before the delivery of 3101–3111 in May 1948. Deliveries from Brush were quite quick and regular, with three more arriving in June 1948, ten more in July, thirteen in August and six in September, while the final six were put into traffic in October 1948.

Unfortunately for Midland Red, while Brush had spare capacity at their works at Loughborough, the delays at Metro-Cammell were protracted because of other large specialised orders – for example, to Birmingham City Transport and London Transport. These other commitments and bodying the S6, S8 and S9 single-deckers for Midland Red, caused the AD2 order to be put 'on the back burner', with, frustratingly for Midland Red, dozens of AEC Regent II chassis being stored as they waited for a bodying slot to become available at Elmdon.

The Metro-Cammell batch of AD2s were numbered 3150–99 (JHA 51–100). The first bus to be delivered was 3160 (JHA 61), arriving in August 1949, but the next three, 3153–4 and 3156, didn't come until March 1950. Fourteen more were delivered in April of the same year but, after that, the remaining buses came in virtually 'penny numbers' throughout the remaining months of 1950, leaving 3188 and 3194 to be the last to enter service in December 1950. Thus these last fifty AD2s had the dubious distinction of being the last Regent IIs to enter service in this country.

One hundred new, albeit non-standard, double-deckers must have been thought of as 'the answer to a maiden's prayer' by the traffic department of Midland Red, who were getting quite tight on double-deck numbers for their intensive urban services in and around Birmingham and the Black Country. Unfortunately it quickly became apparent that these buses were not only late in delivery but were barely up to their intended service requirements as at 7 tons 10 cwt 2 qtr, for both the Brush and Metro-Cammell bodied buses the AD2s the power-to-weight ratio with the AEC 7.57 litre engine was not good. This was quickly revealed when the first ten or so of the Brush-bodied ones were put on the 130 route between Birmingham and Stourbridge, which was then regarded as one of the more important services in the West Midlands. The AD2s could not cope with the heavy loadings and the fearsome climb up the ⅔-mile-long Mucklow Hill, which climbed from 383 feet from the River Stour Valley in Halesowen to 668 feet at the top on the Birmingham Plateau, averaging about 1 in 11, with short sections of 1 in 8. The buses did not survive for many months on the 130 route and the service reverted to the pre-war FEDDs until the arrival of the Leyland-bodied Leyland Titan PD2/12s of 1953. The well-appointed AD2s were quickly put onto less arduous duties, and steep hills and services around Dudley and Oldbury were henceforth avoided.

During their service lives, the modifications to the buses involved raising the top of the recessed windscreen for the benefit of tall drivers. This resulted in the destination winding gear being moved from the inside the cab to an external handle under the canopy next to the cab. A step then had to be fitted into the front grill so that conductors could reach the winding handle! Quite early on in their careers the lack of ventilation in the upper saloon was a cause for concern. 3116 and 3177 were fitted with quite near front hopper ventilators in the front saloon windows, but a pair of fixed vents fitted into the front dome on all the AD2s and the problem was solved.

When new the first Brush-bodied AD2s were allocated to Digbeth Garage in Birmingham but, after their relative failure on the 130 route, these were quickly moved away. Harts Hill in Brierley Hill always had a small number of AD2s, as did Kidderminster. Elsewhere in the Black Country, Oldbury Garage had some for a short time, but their lack of power on the hilly local terrain saw them removed by the mid-1950s. Stourbridge Garage had an allocation of AD2s from 1948 until the early 1960s, while Bilston Street, Wolverhampton, operated few.

Away from the core operating area in the West Midlands, Tamworth and the original Leamington Garage at Old Warwick Road had batches of AD2s from new. Fifteen AD2s were allocated to Emscote Garage in Warwick, where they were to be found on less demanding rural Warwickshire services. The two Leicester garages had examples of both Brush and Metro-Cammell bodies to work on the intense urban services in and around that city. In more rural areas, Banbury, Evesham, Ludlow, Swadlincote garages had AD2s, while the town services in Hereford, Shrewsbury and Stafford were each allocated these Regent IIs. The first double-deckers allocated to Hinckley Garage in 1950 were AD2s, which eventually comprised that garage's entire double-decker fleet, ultimately numbering sixteen vehicles.

The withdrawal of the AD2s took place over just three years. In 1961, nineteen Brush and four MCCW buses were taken out of service. In 1962, twenty-three Brush and twenty-one MCCW went and, finally, in 1963 eight Brush and twenty-five MCCW were retired. That wasn't quite the end, as at least six AD2s – 3100/23/27/45–6 and 3149 – were used as trainee vehicles, usually from Bearwood Garage.

The AD2s were something of a disappointment. They were Midland Red's penultimate class of 7-foot 6-inch-wide double-deckers. With their concealed radiators and four-bay construction bodies, the AD2s looked modern enough, but beneath the surface they were basically a modified pre-war chassis with a small-sized underpowered engine coupled to a heavyweight body.

The Missing AD3 and AD4s

A class of eight AEC Regent III 0961 RT types, to be designated AD3, were to have been ordered with fleet numbers 3300–3307. These would have had the large 9.6-litre engine, coupled to an air-operated pre-selector gearbox and fitted with air brakes. The specification was a little advanced and their purchase was not sanctioned by the management of Midland Red. Just as the Brush-bodied, concealed radiator RT was stillborn, so the BMMO D4, a homemade 8-foot-wide vehicle, never got beyond the drawing board at Carlyle Road.

3100, JHA 1
Twelve brand-new, sparklingly painted AEC Regent II 0661s with Brush H30/26R bodies have been lined up in echelon in 1948. Their destination boxes have been wound on to show the terminal points of the 130 route, with those on the right showing Stourbridge via Halesowen, and those on the left displaying Birmingham via Halesowen. When new these buses worked on the 130 route but, with their small 7.57-litre engines, were not able to keep time especially on the long, steep Mucklow Hill section and the route soon reverted to pre-war FEDDs. The AEC Regent II's normal appearance had been drastically altered by the stylish D1 type enclosed bonnet, yet these AD2 class buses were hardly any advance on the 'unfrozen' Coventry style Regents of 1942. (D. R. Harvey collection)

3149, JHA 50

Above: Travelling along Corporation Street towards Old Square *c.* 1962 is 3149, (JHA 50). This AD2 type bus was an AEC Regent II with a Brush H30/26R body that had been allocated to Hereford Garage for eight years until it was finally withdrawn in March 1961. It was a bus with quite a low mileage and, as such, was chosen to become a staff bus and driver training vehicle, a role it fulfilled for two years. These buses had taken over driver training duties from the last of the SOS FEDDs, a few of which had soldiered on until 1961. With an L plate and the legend 'Trainee Vehicle' in the front lower saloon window, and a suitably stern, regimental driving instructor, the poor learner was thrown into the deep end and given a week to master the joys of a crash gearbox! (R. H. G. Simpson)

3109, JHA 10

Opposite above: Turning out of Hill Street into Victoria Square in front of the Galloway's Corner block of shops and offices in December 1948 is 3109, (JHA 10). This Brush-bodied bus is being used on the 130 service to Halesowen and Stourbridge. There were 100 of these buses, which had the unique chassis AEC Regent II classification of 0661/20, signifying that the chassis had been modified in order to be fitted with the concealed radiator and bonnet assembly. When delivered in April 1948, the top of the recessed windscreen was level with the bottom of the canopy, but such was the driving position that the windscreen was later raised some 3 inches to improve the driver's view, a modification also found on the BMMO D5 and D5Bs. (D. R. Harvey collection)

3126, JHA 27

Opposite below: 3126, (JHA 27), a Brush-bodied AEC Regent 0661, spent all of its operational life from August 1948 until November 1962 working from Leicester's Sandacre Garage. They obviously weren't put off by the tardy performance of the AEC 7.57-litre engine coupled to the 7 ton 10 cwt all-up weight, as it has just arrived in St Margaret's Bus Station parking area, having worked on the X68 service from Birmingham and Coventry. It carries the early 1950s advertisement 'Say CWS and Save'. (D. R. Harvey collection)

3162, JHA 63

3162, (JHA 63) is working on the 554 route from Leamington Spa on the fairly straight run through rural Warwickshire by way of Harbury Lane and Chesterton Road to Harbury and Bishops Itchington. It was an AEC Regent II with a Metro-Cammell H30/26R body that had entered service in April 1950. This route was operated by Leamington Garage, where 3162 was stabled from 1951 until May 1953. By now fitted with the front dome ventilators, 3162 does look in need of a repaint, especially around the concealed radiator area. (J. Fozard)

3194, JHA 95

By the time Metro-Cammell were able to body their part of the fifty AEC Regent IIs, the chassis were nearly four years out of date when 3194 was delivered in December 1950, one of the last AD2s to be so. Standing outside R. R. Hall's fish merchant shop in about 1951 in Leamington Spa town centre is (JHA 95), an AEC Regent II with a crash gearbox and a fifty-six-seater Metro-Cammell body when almost new. 3194 has yet to have the top of its windscreen raised, has no front dome fixed ventilators and is still lined out with yellow lining and contrasting black wings. It is working on the 518 route to Stratford via Wellesbourne Mountford and Warwick. (P. Kingston)

At last – The Homemade D5 and D5Bs

BMMO D5

In early 1949, the first of the new post-war double-decker BMMO chassis had at last been completed. Designated D5, the initial order was for 100 buses equipped with the BMMO 8.028-litre engine and coupled to a four-speed constant-mesh gearbox mounted in the chassis frame rather than in the more usual position immediately behind the engine. The H30/26R body layout of the vehicles was an 8-foot-wide development of the 1944 Weymann-bodied prototype D1, although the body contract was awarded to Brush, whose four-bay open platform rear entrance bodywork was very similar to the bodies fitted to the AEC Regent IIs and given to 3100–3149 in 1948. The D5s were numbered 3457–556 (MHA 457–556). They were quiet and sweet-running buses and gave the passengers a most comfortable ride. Other than their width, these 8-foot-wide buses could also be distinguished from the AD2s by having eight sliding ventilators in each saloon. At the rear, the D5s were fitted with a single triple track destination number box above the open rear platform, where there was an angled staircase. This was not desperately steep, but landed quite close to the platform edge. They had an unladen weight of 7 tons 15 cwt 2 qtrs and so their power-to-weight ratio was similar to the AD2s'.

The early post-war AEC Regent II AD2s and the homemade BMMO D5s and D5Bs lost the pre-war Midland Red philosophy that big engines and lightweight bodywork are a better option than small engines and heavyweight bodywork. The result was that, by 1952, the company had a fleet of 300 double-deckers buses that had little maintenance problems and retained a good fuel consumption, but struggled to keep time on anything other than flat terrain! It would only be with the advent of the under-rated BMMO D7 with lightweight Metro-Cammell bodywork weighing in around 7.25 tons that the old Midland Red thinking re-emerged.

The first of the 100 BMMO D5 double-deck buses, 3457–3465, entered service in July 1949 and were followed in August 1949 by 3466–3526. There was a long gap before 3527–3555 arrived in January 1950, while the last D5 arrived in May 1950. There were a number of vehicles that had obvious modifications. When new, 3553 was fitted with a radiator grill that was similar to the centre grill from a Birmingham New Look fronted bus. Similarly, 3504 entered service with a prototype grill that was later adopted for the later D7 model. As with the bodies on the AD2s, these buses had a ventilation problem in the upper saloon; 3478 was fitted with a pair of opening ventilators, but these were not satisfactory and the whole class was fitted with a pair of open hoppers in the front dome, giving the front of the bus a look akin to a pair of surprised eyebrows above the curved profile of the depressed-looking upper saloon windows. 3498 was fitted with a prototype offside fluorescent advertisement panel in about 1959.

The allocation of these D5s were mainly in the West Midlands and Leicester urban areas, though about one third of the class were scattered around the more rural cathedral cities, market towns and regional centres across the huge Midland Red operating area. The D5s were intended for urban work in the Birmingham and Black Country, and so Digbeth Garage received BMMO D5s in about 1952, while Sheepcote Street, off Broad Street in Birmingham, which opened on 19 August 1951, had up to twenty of the class. Harts Hill and Oldbury garages each had over twenty D5s. With their open platforms, the D5s were well suited to the intensive urban services between Birmingham, Smethwick, Oldbury and Dudley, and the routes between Oldbury and West Bromwich. Bilston Street Garage in Wolverhampton also intermittently operated D5s.

Outside the West Midlands conurbation, Kidderminster operated a small fleet of D5s while, in 1949, a dozen D5s were sent to Redditch Garage, replacing early SOS FEDDs. Sutton Coldfield's numerous urban services both within the Royal Burgh and on the many routes to Birmingham meant that up to twenty-plus D5s were allocated to the town garage. In the East Midlands, Southgate Street, Leicester operated some twenty-five D5s while Coalville also had about six D5s.

The first withdrawals took place in 1962, when 3495/99/3507–8/10/21–22 and 3548 were taken out of service after the introduction of Daimler Fleetlines and BMMO D9s in 1963 ravaged the class. In 1963 another fifty-six of the class went for scrap, while in 1964 the stock of D5s was diminished by twenty-three, leaving just a dozen in stock at the start of 1965. By 1966 only 3484, 3519 and 3555 were in service. Three buses, 3467, 3480 and 3492, were briefly used as trainers at the Driving School, while 3508 was converted to a tree-lopper for use at Leamington Spa Garage.

3460, MHA 460
Opposite above: The first 8-foot-wide double-deckers in the Midland Red fleet were their own, long-awaited BMMO D5 model. The attractive Brush H30/26R bodywork was based on those built on the AEC Regent 0661 AD2 class, but had sliding ventilators in each saloon window. 3460, (MHA 460), entered service in August 1949 and would stay in service for exactly fifteen years. It is parked alongside Burleys Way in St Margaret's Bus Station in about 1957. It was allocated to Southgate Street Garage and has been working on the busy L8 route from South Wigston. (R. H. G. Simpson)

3478, MHA 478
Opposite below: 3478, (MHA 478), was new in December 1949 and was fitted with opening ventilators in front upper-deck windows from new, which quite suited the rest of the body design. 3478 retained these ventilators until it was withdrawn in May 1963. The bus is climbing Rose Hill on its way over Lickey Hill, which reaches 978 feet above sea level. The Brush four-bay bodywork really suited the BMMO D5, although the design of the multi-slatted radiator grill looked a little fussy and was the subject of numerous experimental potential replacements. Despite their lack of doors, when new the D5s were used on long-distance routes such as the 143 route, which travelled the length of Bristol Road to the tram terminus at Rednal before undertaking this steep climb and then dropping down into Bromsgrove on a journey that took 45 minutes. While inside the Birmingham boundary, under the terms of the 1914 Agreement with Birmingham Corporation, passengers on services that operated from the city centre could only be picked up at certain points – in this case at Oak Tree Lane, Selly Oak and The Bell at Northfield. (M. Rooum)

3506, MHA 506

Many bus services running south from Birmingham started on the setts in front of St Martin's Parish Church in the Bull Ring. Brush-bodied D5 3506 entered service in October 1949 and is still quite new, though fitted with fixed ventilator slots in the front dome. It is about to leave on the 155 to Solihull by way of Warwick Road, Acocks Green and Olton on an appallingly wet day. St Martin's churchyard is to the right of the bus behind the trees. Behind the bus are some of the buildings that survived the wartime bombing, which affected this area of the city centre so badly. The bus survived in service until September 1964. (M. Rooum)

3551, MHA 551

Parked in Dudley Bus Station is one of Cradley Heath Garage's Brush H30/26R-bodied BMMO D5s. 3551, (MHA 551), was delivered to Digbeth Garage in March 1950 and stayed there until it was moved to Cradley Heath in July 1962. It is seen during the summer of 1963 when resting after being used on the 243 service from Cradley Heath to Dudley by way of Old Hill and Netherton. This sojourn in the Black Country was quite brief as 3551 was withdrawn in May 1964. The BMMO D5s were the last buses delivered to Midland Red with open rear platforms. (P. Yeomans)

D5B

The second batch of BMMO buses were designated by BMMO with the code D5B and were numbered 3777–876 (NHA 777–876). Mechanically identical to the D5, the 100 D5Bs were something of a trendsetter as they were built with rear platform doors and had enclosed rear platform fitted with electrically operated four-leaf folding rear entrance doors based on the 1949 modification developed on the D1 2541. They had an emergency door fitted at the bottom of the staircase on the rear wall of the vehicle – a legal requirement on vehicles with platform doors. Other notable changes to this second batch of vehicles included saloon heaters, improved seating and a different radiator grille. The weight of the vehicles at 7 tons 19½ cwt was a quarter of a ton heavier than their earlier open-platform cousins. The enclosed platforms made them ideal for the longer interurban services rather than the short-haul routes in the West Midlands.

The performance of the D5Bs was sedate rather than sparkling. They were used as front-line service buses across the whole of the Midland Red operating area but, just like the AD2s, were not really suited to the hillier Black Country services. In 1956, using 3874 as a testbed, perhaps in preparation for the forthcoming D9 rather than to upgrade the D5B's performance, it was fitted with the new BMMO 10.5-litre engine operating from Bearwood and Cradley Heath garages until 1958, when it reverted to normal. A later modification occurred with 3839, which was fitted with a supercharged version of the 8.028-litre engine in December 1963. 3872 was sent to Leyland Motors in January 1952 in order to act as a template for the design of the concealed radiator, which Midland Red had specified on their order for 100 Titan PD2/12s.

Deliveries of the D5B began only thee months after the final D5. The first D5B to enter service was 3777, which arrived in August 1950; this was some two months before 3778–3780 and 3784, which entered service in October 1950. By the end of the year deliveries from the Loughborough bodybuilder had reached 3809. Throughout 1951, the BMMO D5Bs continued to arrive at a rate of between six and eleven per month, reaching 3869 by the end of the year. The final bus to be delivered was 3873, which began its service life in April 1952, becoming one of the last Brush-built double-deckers to be constructed before coachbuilding ceased.

Once in service, the D5Bs were largely left unmodified. 3783 was equipped with a pair of opening ventilators in the front windows, but the whole class was fitted with a pair of front dome open hoppers as was retrospectively fitted to the AD2 and D5 vehicles. In 1956, 3852 was converted to an H33/26RD, but this was the only one so modified.

Initially, Digbeth Garage received twenty-three D5Bs, while Oldbury also operated a sizeable fleet. The long routes from Wolverhampton to Stourbridge were ideally suited to the doored D5Bs and, as a result, Stourbridge Garage received D5Bs. Sutton Coldfield Garage had D5Bs for their town services. Evesham Hereford and Kidderminster garages each had half a dozen D5Bs while, in 1951, twelve of the class were allocated to Redditch Garage. Sandacre Street, Leicester, operated up to a dozen D5Bs.

Withdrawals began in 1962, when 3873 was not repaired after an accident. In 1963 there were just five D5Bs withdrawals and thirteen in the following year. Over the next three years there was a complete obliteration of these attractive buses, as they were decimated by the introduction of the advanced BMMO D9s. Twenty-two withdrawals occurred in 1965; in 1966 thirty-three D5Bs went; and, finally, in 1967 the last twenty-six were withdrawn. 3798 and 3873 were briefly used as trainee buses by the Carlyle Road's Training School, while 3787 was cut down to upper saloon floor level to become a tree-lopper, a role it fulfilled from 1965 until 1969.

The only survivor was 3795, which entered service in 1951 and spent its life allocated to Sutton Coldfield, Hinckley, Tamworth and Wigston before it was delicensed in July 1964. It was sold without running units to Hednesford Hills Raceway, where it was used as the scoreboard. It was subsequently purchased by BaMMOT and today is exhibited in an unrestored state.

3788, NHA 788

Above: The fronts of the Brush-bodied BMMO D5Bs and their D5 predecessors were identical, but it was at the rear that the D5Bs had enclosed platforms. 3788, (NHA 788), a D5B stands in front of 3510, (MHA 510), a D5, when both buses are working on the 144 service from Malvern to Birmingham via Worcester. Unlike the D5s, these 100 buses came with the front dome ventilators but still with the low top windscreen. 3788 entered service in November 1950 from Digbeth Garage before moving to Oldbury in February 1959, where it stayed for nearly another seven years before being withdrawn in June 1967. (D. R. Harvey collection)

3796, NHA 796

Opposite above: The Brush-bodied BMMO D5Bs owed their platform doors to the rebuilding of the BMMO D1 in 1949 with this feature. This gave these buses a certain level of luxury and was able to keep the bus warmer for long-distance passengers. However, as they weighed a quarter of a ton more than the D5s, the performance of these buses, with their BMMO 8.028-litre engines, tended to be comfortable rather than speedy. These buses were well appointed and gave a comfortable, if somewhat steady ride for their passengers. Standing in the bus station yard in front of Southgate Street Garage is 3796, (NHA 796), one of their own allocation of D5Bs. In September 1951, this nine-month-old bus is waiting to leave on the long X68 service to Coventry and Birmingham, which took 2 hours and 8 minutes. (G. H. F. Atkins)

3826, NHA 826

3826, (NHA 826), is in Shrewsbury Bus Station and is waiting for its next trip on the S1 town service. In the distance is 4697, 697 BHA, a BMMO S14 converted to OMO, while beyond that is a 36-foot-long Willowbrook-bodied Leyland Leopard PSU3/4R. This BMMO D5B arrived in Shrewsbury in July 1955 and remained in the town until it was taken out of service in March 1964. The bus is in its last year of service, as passing it is a Triumph Herald dating from 1963. (A. D. Broughall)

3859, NHA 859

Working on the S19 town service to Bayston Hill in Shrewsbury is BMMO D5B 3859, (NHA 859). These were the first buses in the fleet to have enclosed rear platforms. On the Brush bodies the enclosed platform was particularly neatly done, with an emergency exit door in the back wall of the bus. The bus entered service in September 1951 and within a month went to Shrewsbury Garage, where it stayed for most of its life. (A. D. Broughall)

3876, NHA 876

The final D5B was 3876, (NHA 876), which was delivered in February 1952 to Kidderminster Garage, on whose 133 Stourport service it is about to operate. The bus is parked in Worcester Street in Birmingham, in front of the premises of the Coventry Lever Co., who were watchmakers. The bus had the 'Crawford's Cream Cracker' advertisement, which was common on Midland Red buses from about 1953 for the next four years. These BMMO D5B buses were the last double-deck Brush bodies built for Midland Red prior to that coachbuilder's cessation of body building at the beginning of June 1952. (D. R. Harvey collection)

GD6

During the late 1940s Midland Red's management realised that further buses would have to be purchased 'off-the-peg' from an outside manufacturer. During the Second World War, the Ministry of War Transport allocated fifty-seven Guy Arabs to Midland Red. These simple, robust vehicles had obviously impressed the BMMO management and so Guy Motors was approached to supply twenty complete vehicles specifically for the services in and around Dudley. In 1949 Midland Red ordered twenty Guy Arab III chassis fitted a constant mesh gearbox coupled to the powerful and compact Meadows 6CD 10.35-litre engine; this unit was developed as a prototype in 1945 and offered by Guys between 1948 and 1951. The Henry Meadows factory was in Cannock Road, Wolverhampton, next door to Guy's Fallings Park Works, and Meadows supplied the 6CD unit for the Arab III chassis. The new Arab III model had a lower radiator position virtually flush to the cab's front apron that was only 5 feet at the filler cap, which not only looked better but gave the driver a clear view of the road.

In 1947 Guy came to an agreement with Park Royal that enabled it to build Park Royal-designed bodies under licence. Chassis were sent to London, where the frames, manufactured by Metal Sections of Oldbury, were built on to the chassis and the bus was driven back in skeletal form to Wolverhampton for panelling and trimming. They had the standard H30/26R bodies with four half-drop ventilators in the lower saloon and six in the upper saloon, and a steep, angled staircase weighing just over 7½ tons. These open platform buses were quite basic, lacking twin-skinned ceilings in the upper saloon, lined interior panelling or heaters. They were painted in a gold-lined all-over red livery with black front and rear wings. Midland Red's twenty buses were ordered in 1948 and classified GD6 (Guy Double-decker), becoming the last 7-foot 6-inch-wide and exposed radiator double-deckers buses to be purchased. The Guys were allocated fleet numbers 3557–76, with near-matching registrations MHA 57–76. The first four were delivered between 31 March and 8 April 1949 and, by 5 July 1949, the first ten were in service. The last one, 3576, arrived at Carlyle Road Works on 17 November 1949.

Dudley, in the heart of the Black Country, had some fearsome hills within the operating area of the town's Midland Red garage. Strangely, the Dudley drivers hadn't any experience with the earlier wartime Guys, so these somewhat basic-looking buses with the exposed radiators with Guy's feathered head-dressed Indian head mounted atop the filler cap must have made a few hearts sink on first impression. Yet, with their high power-to-weight ratio, they stormed around the hilly Dudley area services with contemptuous ease. Once the drivers had gotten used to their four-speed constant-mesh gearboxes, they found them straightforward to drive. The deep, refined roar of the Meadows engine and loud exhaust note became a regular sound on the local services and, with their excellent turn of speed, were used to great advantage on the 125 inter-urban route between Birmingham and Wolverhampton via Dudley, using the Birmingham New Road. The 140 route from Birmingham to Dudley by way of Blackheath and Rowley Regis had one majestic climb up to Rowley Top Church from Blackheath, of which the GD6s were masters. Then there was the D10 route from the Lodge Farm Estate with its long 1-in-7 climb to Netherton Parish Church. Even Dudley Bus Station, in Birmingham Street, was built on the side of Castle Hill, frequently causing difficulties with normal starts let alone 'three-bell' loads.

The 10.35-litre-engined double-deckers had a bottom-end torque that would put an elephant to shame, and they all operated on routes where a 1 in 9 climb were regarded as normal! The problem was that all that power from their non-standard engines on the steep hills reduced the fuel consumption figures alarmingly. When new these Meadows-engined post-war Guys had transformed Dudley Garage's route timings but their very success was their Achilles' heel. The Meadows unit was effectively too big, too thirsty and too unusual to stand much of a chance in just twenty double-decker buses whose engines had many of the essential auxiliaries located on the 'wrong side' for easy maintenance.

Around the time of their first overhaul, in 1952, 3558 had been tried out with a Gardner 5LW 7.0-litre engine, prompting unrepeatable comments from the drivers at Dudley! Mercifully this was a one-off, but the die had been cast and, later in 1952, all the Meadows engines were taken out and replaced by BMMO K type direct injection 8.028-litre oil units. It was a very smooth-running engine with flexible engine mountings and was both reliable and frugal. With their newly installed 8.028-litre engines, they were still able to perform well, but had been neutered in the name of fuel economy. The main visual difference, once re-engined with the BMMO K type unit, was that the chrome surround of the radiator stood proud of the cab apron.

In the mid-1950s some quite extensive body rebuilding was undertaken on the GD6s as they gradually rattled themselves to bits on the indifferent Dudley area road surfaces. Roads in this former coal mining area were constantly subsiding and in need of repair due to old abandoned coal workings shifting. At least five GD6s were fitted with rubber-mounted front upper saloon windows and several more had the front rain-strip above the same windows removed. Withdrawal came suddenly; 3567/8 were taken out of service in 1961 and the rest were withdrawn in 1962, all being sold for scrap. The GD6s operated nearly all their lives at Dudley Garage and all had clocked up some 750,000 miles in just over twelve years' arduous service.

There once was an apocryphal tale told about the GD6s. This went that, with a full load, they could pull away from the stop in Birmingham Road outside Dudley Bus Garage and be in top gear halfway up Castle Hill, before turning into the bus station in Birmingham Street. That is why they were such splendid buses!

3559, MHA 59

3559, (MHA 59), of April 1949 is standing in Stourbridge Garage, at the end used as an undercover bus station. It has just completed the long 'tour' of the Black Country, working on the 245 service and taking in Amblecote, Brierley Hill, Dudley, Tipton, and Ocker Hill before arriving some 62 minutes later in Wednesbury. By now fitted with a BMMO K type engine, but showing no evidence of any body rebuilding around the upper saloon front windows, it would last until October 1962. (D. R. Harvey collection)

3560, MHA 60

The home of the GD6s was Dudley. Most of the town's local services started in the bus station located in Birmingham Street. Unfortunately the station was located on a steep hill, which frequently caused problems, especially in wintery weather. Park Royal H30/26R-bodied Guy Arab III 3560, (MHA 60), entered service in November 1949 and spent its entire working life based at Dudley Garage. It is working on the D11 route to the Priory Estate, while behind it is 3569, (MHA 69), which is being used in the D12 service. By this time both buses had been re-engined with BMMO K type units, with their radiators standing proud of the cab apron. (R. F. Mack)

3564, MHA 64

In its original condition, with the large Meadows 6DC 10.35-litre engine, 3564, (MHA 64), dating from June 1949, is changing its crew at Dudley Garage. It is working on the 120 service from Birmingham via Oldbury. This Guy Arab IIIs Guy-finished Park Royal-framed H30/26R body looks as though it would need a good wash at the end of the day. These powerful buses, with fairly lightweight bodywork, were bought 'off-the-peg' specifically for the routes around Dudley, which had notoriously steep climbs. The 'Mighty' GD6s were comfortably able to cope and ruled the Dudley services for about twelve years, though latterly with the smaller but more economically viable BMMO K 8.028-litre engine during 1952. 3564 was one of the last six GD6s to be withdrawn in December 1962. (D. R. Harvey collection)

3573, MHA 73

The conductress leans against the nearside front wing of the almost new 3573, (MHA 73). This Guy Arab III with a Guy/Park Royal H30/26R body entered service in October 1949 and has just arrived outside Birmingham's florally bedecked Museum and Art Gallery on the 140 service from Dudley in about 1951. It is carrying an advertisement for Turog, which confusingly was a type of brown bread and not a brand of tea as suggested by the slogan. (M. Rooum)

Leyland LD8s

By the early 1950s, the next Midland Red Carlyle Road-built double-decker was still some time away while Brush Engineering of Loughborough, their regular supplier of bus bodies since the 1920s, were completing their final orders prior to ceasing coachbuilding. Yet again the company would have to look elsewhere for a substantial number of new double-deck buses, which were beginning to be urgently required as traffic requirements were rapidly increasing.

Whether it was the success of the thirteen Leyland-bodied Leyland Titan PD2/1s bought by their Stratford Blue subsidiary in 1948 and 1950 is open to question, but their excellent performance, fuel economy and reliability must have had an influence on the parent company's decision to approach Leyland Motors for 100 new buses. The new PD2/12 chassis had been developed in 1950, first appearing as Leicester City Transport's 160 (FJF 199) and was 27 feet long and 8 inches wide with a 16-foot 5-inch wheelbase. It had the powerful Leyland o.600 9.8-litre engine, delivering 125 bhp at 1,800 rpm and coupled to a four-speed gearbox with synchromesh on second, third and fourth gears and had vacuum brakes.

Since 1944 Midland Red had built their conventional vertical front-engined-chassis D1, AD2, D5 and D5B but with their pioneering 'in house'-designed concealed radiator, front grille and bonnet assembly. In January 1952, with the prospect of a large order from Midland Red for their new PD2/12 model, Leyland Motors borrowed Brush-bodied BMMO D5B 3872 (NHA 872) to use as a template for the concealed full-width front specified by Midland Red, which would enhance the appearance of the Leyland's front.

The Leyland design was a slightly more bulbous profile, but with a more angular, lower profiled bonnet than the BMMO assembly. It had a removable grille with twelve vertical slats, and it had a space at the top for the BMMO badge. The bonnet assembly was fixed to the chassis, with a hinged bonnet cover giving access over the nearside front wing to the engine compartment. The 100 buses built for Midland Red were the only new PD2/12s fitted with this Leyland-built concealed radiator front, although Edinburgh Corporation retrospectively fitted concealed radiators for its fleet of Leyland-bodied PD2/12s. As a result of this special order, Leyland designated the Midland Red buses as PD2/12 Specials. Subsequently this new front assembly was offered by Leyland to other operators as their standard concealed radiator Titans, even retaining the space intended for the BMMO badge. The 8-foot-wide Leyland H30/26RD metal-framed body tapered inwards to a 7-foot 6-inch-wide front, making the new concealed radiator assembly suitable for both available body widths.

Most drivers enjoyed the performance of the Leylands but conductors found that their soft springs and ability to pitch over on sharp corners made it difficult to collect fares and issue tickets. The buses were all fitted with heaters, with the lower saloon ducting occupying the centre pillar of the front bulkhead. Passengers, however, could find the LD8s less than comfortable due to their low-backed brown rexine seats and small number of saloon stanchions.

The 'final Leyland design' was probably one of the best-looking half-cab double-deck bodies ever built. The new Leyland PD2/12 double-deck body had a five-bay layout, and a new style of glazing with pressed window radiused pans and sliding windows incorporated into the main outline of the windows. Inside the buses there was attractively pressed window mouldings, while in the upper saloon the front and rear domes were double-skinned. When Leyland placed the Midland Red design of a concealed radiator Titan into production later in 1953 it was redesignated as a PD2/20.

The 100 PD2/12 specials were numbered 3978–4077 (SHA 378-477) and were classified by Midland Red as their LD8 class (Leyland Double-decker type 8). The first bus, 3978 (SHA 978), was exhibited at the Earl's Court Commercial Motor Show in November 1952 and differed from the rest of the class by having front dome ventilators, à la those on the D5Bs, and only six sliding ventilators in the lower deck rather than the normal eight. A pair of vertical ventilators was fitted in the rear upper saloon side windows. The Leyland body had platform doors and an emergency door at the back of the platform, while in the upper saloon the emergency window had the final shallow design of Leyland's two-piece window, only supplied to Plymouth Corporation and Trent Motor Traction. The LD8s Leyland body uniquely had the offside cab window level with the bottom of the door in order to marry up with the bottom corner of the recessed opening windscreen.

Only 3978 and 4017, both used for official photographs, were fitted with rear wheel discs but, when new, all the buses had front wheel nut guard rings. The buses weighed 8 tons 2 cwts. When delivered, the LD8s were painted in all-over red with three thin yellow lines below each saloon's windows and one at upper saloon floor level and black painted wings. Quite a number carried painted advertisements for 'CRAWFORD'S CREAM CRACKERS' and 'ATKINSON'S ALES', which actually enhanced the appearance of these buses. After 3978 was delivered in November 1952, after the Earl's Court exhibition, 3979–4005 arrived during January 1953 and the final two buses arrived in June of that year.

Many LD8s were allocated to garages in the West Midlands. Thirty-three of them were new to Digbeth Garage, with many spending their entire service lives there. They were well-suited to the numerous long and fast routes operated from Digbeth, where their powerful engines and the synchromesh gearboxes were much appreciated. Routes such as the 125 between Birmingham and Wolverhampton, the 150 to Stratford, the 159 between Birmingham and Coventry and the 184 route to Warwick were favoured haunts of these buses for virtually all their working lives. The LD8s made an interesting contrast with the three Stratford Blue Leyland-bodied exposed radiator Leyland Titan PD2/12s, 23–25 (MAC 570–572), which shared the duties on the prestigious Birmingham–Stratford-upon-Avon route. Eighteen of the earliest LD8s were allocated to Bearwood Garage in 1953 and were rather unpopular on some of the routes around Smethwick and Halesowen, where their 'long-striding' performance and soft suspension was not suited to the tight turns on the routes running around inter-war housing estates. In the Black Country, Oldbury Garage had some of its fleet of AD2s replaced in 1953 by ten of the powerful Leylands, while Wolverhampton had a small number to operate on the 125 route between Birmingham and Wolverhampton. Harts Hill Garage in Brierley Hill had ten LD8s, while Upper Holland Street in Sutton Coldfield had the occasional allocation of LD8s.

Kidderminster and Ludlow garages each were provided with the formidable LD8s to operate on the long and seriously hilly 192 service to Ludlow from Birmingham over Clee Hill. They were also used on the 60-mile long X34 and X35 group of services, the longest double-decker route operated by Midland Red, which mainly followed the A49 between Shrewsbury and Hereford via Church Stretton, Craven Arms, Ludlow and Leominster. The old Leamington & Warwick Tramways depot in Emscote, Warwick, also had around fifteen LD8s sent there from new and these went to Leamington Spa when the new garage opened in September 1957, working on the 517 service to Coventry and the 518 service to Warwick and Stratford.

The impression of the LD8 buses operated by the Black Country garages was that their performance lacked sparkle. This possibly was due to the torpedo-type air filter fitted to some of these buses, giving them a totally different sound to Leylands operating elsewhere, which took the edge off their running – elsewhere they were 'real fliers'. In their early years their synchromesh gearboxes were prone to failure, resulting in Leyland providing new GB83 gearboxes with synchromesh on just third and fourth gears. The result was a far more robust and reliable gearbox, but at the cost of alienating some of the Midland Red drivers due to the loss of synchromesh on second gear. A lesser problem was that they were not fitted with flashing indicators until their last years.

As with so many types of Midland Red double-deckers, their withdrawal was quick and ruthless. The first ten LD8s were withdrawn in 1965, while some seventy-two buses were taken out of service in 1966, before the type was eliminated in 1967 with the withdrawal of the remaining eighteen buses. Two LD8s, 4048 and 4055, were acquired by G&G Coaches of Leamington in January 1966, with 4055 lasting until August 1972. Ironically G&G used them on the same 517 service that they had previously worked on for Midland Red between Leamington Spa and Coventry. The Londonderry & Lough Swilly Railway purchased 4014, 4019, 4021 and 4066, and they proved to be excellent purchases, lasting in service until 1976. 4004 and 4037 were sold to Lesney, the manufacturers of Matchbox Models, as staff transport. 4031 and 4035 were sold to Foster Brothers, the Solihull-based gentlemen's outfitters for staff transport. After years of patient and extensive restoration by the 1685 Group based at BaMMOT, Wythall, 4031 was finally restored to its original glory in the summer of 2010 and it looks absolutely stunning.

3978, SHA 378

In November 1952, straight from that year's Commercial Motor Show, the first LD8, 3978, (SHA 378), stands in the slush in Navigation Street, which is rather spoiling its pristine condition. The Queen's Hotel looms imposingly behind the brand-new Leyland, which was the first Leyland vehicle fitted with their version of the BMMO D5B bonnet assembly. 3978 is working on the 133 route to Stourport via Kidderminster, where its Leyland 0.600 9.8-litre engine's power could be used to the full. Of all 100 LD8s, this Leyland Titan PD2/12's Leyland H30/26RD body was the only one to sport fixed ventilators in the front dome. (R. Knibbs)

3990, SHA 390

The LD8s were ideally suited to long, fast runs and, with their synchromesh gearboxes, were easy to drive. The long X35 route was one such route that was ideal for these Leyland-bodied Leyland Titan PD2/12s. Running from Shrewsbury to Hereford by way of Church Stretton, Ludlow and Leominster, the journey time was 2 hours 50 minutes. The driver of 3990, (SHA 390), is taking a short break before continuing the journey to Hereford *c.* 1960, by which time the spray-painting reduced the buses to an all-over red livery with no relief colouring. (R. Marshall)

4025, SHA 425

A rather dusty 4025, (SHA 425), travels through Sparkbrook in Birmingham while working the 23-mile-long 150 route to Stratford-upon-Avon via Henley-in-Arden. This service was also operated by Stratford Blue Motors. These Midland Red vehicles had the round cornered window pans that characterised the last few years of Leyland double-deck bodywork design. The 3978-4077 class was built with a front end design specified by Midland Red. They were the only Leyland-bodied buses to have this front from new, which was coupled with a recessed windscreen. (S. N. J. White)

4035, SHA 435

Travelling along Belvoir Street in Leicester and passing the headquarters of the Leicester branch of the Civil Defence Corps is 4035, (SHA 435). This Leyland-bodied Leyland Titan PD2/12 is working on the X68 route when newly resprayed in all-over red in the mid-1950s, though it does look extremely smart despite losing its black painted wings. This bus entered service at Digbeth Garage in March 1953 and spent almost all its life there, not being withdrawn until September 1966. (D. R. Harvey Collection)

4057, SHA 457

Above: The initial livery for the LD8s was overall red with gold 'Midland' fleetnames and pinstripe lining, with black wheel arches and window surrounds, all of which looked extremely smart. Throughout its life, 4057, (SHA 457), new in April 1953, was always allocated to Leamington Garage, where it remained until September 1966. The bus has turned out of Tiddington Road in front of the sixteenth-century Alveston Manor Hotel and on to the approach to the fifteenth-century Clopton Bridge over the River Avon in about 1953. Waiting to follow the bus is a 1951 Ford Consul EOTA, just beyond the young lady cyclist. (D. R. Harvey Collection)

4039, SHA 439

Opposite above: 4039, (SHA 439), has just arrived in Pool Meadow Bus Station and, having disgorged its passengers, the crew have parked up their bus and gone for a well-earned break. This Leyland-bodied Leyland Titan PD2/12 is working on the less-than-common 588 route from Leamington to Coventry but via Stoneleigh in the early 1960s. The cabs on these buses were unique to them as the bottom of the front offside cab window lined up with the saloon windows whereas, on all other Leyland bodies, this window was lower to match the bottom of the windscreen. (R. Weaver)

4040, SHA 440

Opposite below: Despite the loss of its gold lining out, Leyland-bodied Leyland 4040, (SHA 440), still looks extremely smart as it stands on the cobbles on the wrong side of Worcester Street, Birmingham. Behind the bus are the Doric columns of the Market Hall, completed in 1835 to the design of Charles Edge and severely damaged by an incendiary bomb on 25 August 1940. These Leyland Titans are PD2/12s with synchromesh gearbox and vacuum brakes, and fitted with enclosed radiators. It was only after their completion that Leyland Motors classified all concealed radiator PD2/12s as PD2/20s. (S. N. J. White)

BMMO D7s

In August 1953, the first of the new BMMO D7 double-deckers, 4078, (THA 78), entered service. It would be the first of 350 of the model to be operated. The ending of bodybuilding by Brush of Loughborough in 1952 meant that Midland Red had to look for another body manufacturer for these new buses. The chosen coachbuilder was Metro-Cammell, who built a four-bay, metal-framed body to Midland Red's own specification.

Although the D7 had the same 16-foot 3-inch wheelbase as the D5B, it was not just an upgraded D5B as the chassis and engine were different in a number of ways. The D7 was nominally 27 feet long. The chassis frame was slightly modified, to allow the gearbox to be mounted directly on to the engine at the front of the chassis frame, rather than having it remotely mounted, as on the D5 and D5B. The engine was the BMMO 8.028-litre diesel engine, but this was the newly developed KL (Kidney Long) type with a longer crankshaft and larger main bearings. This enabled the engine to produce a better performance from the same cubic capacity. As a result, the BMMO D7 was very reliable and the KL-type engine, coupled with the lightweight body, gave a lively performance that earned the model a fine reputation.

They were the last double-deck vehicles built by BMMO, with a constant-mesh four-speed gearbox. The second, third and fourth ratios had short lever throws into each gear, with first, with its distinctly vintage sound, having a very long travel; once mastered, the gearbox gave a very smooth gear change. A few D7s were used as test beds with 4368 (VHA 368), being fitted with a Self-Changing Gears Two-Pedal control Semi-Automatic gearbox in 1957, operated by a small lever alongside the steering wheel. This arrangement was developed further and used on 4773 (773 FHA), the prototype BMMO D9. In 1957, 4433 was briefly fitted with an air-cooled version of the BMMO KL engine, while December 1963 saw six buses (4084, 4099, 4103, 4162, 4169 and VHA-registered 4369) fitted with turbo-charged BMMO KL 8.028-litre engines.

By choosing Metro-Cammell as the bodybuilder, the Midland Red tradition of having a body built to a lightweight standard was resumed, as the MCCW group were developing their own lightweight Orion style. Whereas the standard Orion body was usually a five-bay construction body with deeper saloon windows in the lower saloon, the bodywork designed for the D7 was of four-bay construction and equal depth windows in each saloon. All four bays in each saloon were fitted with sliding ventilators, while the front windows had pull-in ventilators, abandoning the previous type of front dome fixed vents. The side windows in the rear dome were fitted with vertical push-out ventilators. Like the LD8s and the D5Bs, the D7 was fitted with an enclosed rear platform with electric doors and an emergency platform door.

Although some of the first batch had pop-rivetted panelling, this was soon replaced by conventional joining strips. About halfway through the production run of the 350 buses, the double-skinned fibre-glass front and rear domes were replaced initially by smooth, internally finished domes, but eventually even this was cheapened by domes showing the bare fibre-glass material that was just painted over! This paring down of the specification of the D7 body meant that the early bodies weighed only 7 tons 2 cwt, with the initial seating capacity of H32/26R, which was nearly ¾ ton lighter than the D5Bs. Of these THA-registered D7s, 4083 ran for many years without front-opening ventilators while 4176 uniquely had the route and destination blinds reversed with the number blind being nearest to the pavement in order that passengers could more easily see the route number.

The combination of the improved BMMO KL engine and the lightweight body produced a bus of surprisingly lively performance and an adequate seating capacity. Unfortunately Midland Red wanted to squeeze more seating capacity out of the D7s. The last of the first batch, 4177, entering service in December 1954, was built with an extra row of upper saloon seats, giving it a capacity of 37. This H37/26R layout became the new standard in May 1955 for buses numbered after 4403, though it increased the unladen weight to 7 tons 7 cwt 1qtr.

There were three batches of D7s: the first 100 were numbered 4078–4177 (THA 78–177). 4078 and 4079 entered service in August 1953 shortly after the last of the LD8 buses. Deliveries continued apace until finally 4175–4176 went into service in October 1954, leaving the sole H37/26R example, 4177, to be placed in service in December 1954. The second batch of 200 D7s was equally divided by their registrations, numbered 4353–4452 (VHA 353–452) and 4453–4552 (XHA 453–552). 4353–4377 entered operation in November 1954 and, throughout the rest of 1955, the remainder of the VHA-registered buses reserved by Smethwick CBC in March 1954 were delivered by December 1955. Buses up to 4402 had the lower seating capacity of fifty-eight while those from 4403 onwards were fitted out as sixty-three-seaters. As the earlier D7s were brought back to Carlyle Road Works for overhaul, the lower seating capacity was brought up to the later sixty-three capacity, although somewhat strangely 4400 was overlooked and retained its H32/26RD layout until it was withdrawn. The XHA-registered D7s began to arrive in December 1955, when 4453–4459 entered service. These were followed throughout 1956 by the rest of the batch, with the exception of 4552, which was delivered January 1957.

All of the BMMO D7s as far as 4493 entered service in an all-over red livery with black wings and three gold livery bands below the lower saloon windows, at lower saloon cantrail level and finally below the upper saloon windows. April and May 1956 were transitional months as regards the changeover from the original livery to the much less attractive all-over spray painting of unrelieved red. 4494–4500 arrived in all-over red between April and June 1956, but with the 1944 style of yellow fleet numbers with deep black shading. From 4501, delivered in mid-June 1956, the D7s had thinner, unshaded yellow fleet numbers. One of the first batch of spray-painted D7s, 4499 (XHA 499), was briefly fitted with an S14 grill, but it looked 'wimpish' on the double-decker.

Other odd modifications were on 4452, which had a modified windscreen and a hopper ventilator in the front-facing lower saloon window, while 4456 and 4497 had one-piece destination apertures. 4481 received a D9 type rear platform in the early 1960s after a severe rear-end accident and, from 4503 onwards, the upper saloon front window handrails were reinforced in an attempt to prevent the fibre-glass front domes rattling loose or cracking, with a stress fracture coming from a window corner. Various straps, gussets and other devises were employed to strengthen the domes but the problem inevitably re-occurred. In later years exactly the same problem occurred with the domes on the D9s.

Sandwiched between the prototype C5 coach and the prototype D9 came the final group of fifty D7s, numbered 4723–4772 (723–772 BHA). 4723–4731 entered service in January 1957. Throughout the rest of the year, deliveries of these reverse-BHA-registered D7s came in small numbers until the final bus, 4772, was delivered in October 1957, becoming the last BMMO double-decker to enter service with a 'stick change' gearbox.

For the next decade or more, the D7 was the workhorse of the Midland Red fleet. Although having a rather plain exterior and a utilitarian interior with a lack of legroom in the upper saloon and low-backed seating, they were not an unattractive design, although they were perhaps more popular with the crews than the passengers. Although not as stylish as the earlier D5Bs, the D7 was a reliable bus with a more than lively performance and, in the lower saloon at least, a quite comfortable ride for the passengers. The 350 D7s were an underrated design and were built in greater numbers than either the pre-war SOS FEDD or the D9, their better known successor.

The D7 was found operating throughout the Midland Red area with Birmingham's Digbeth and Sheepcote Street Garages and Cradley Heath, Dudley and Harts Hill in the Black Country all having substantial numbers. Oldbury Garage had about twenty-five D7s used mainly on the B87 service, between Birmingham and Dudley via Smethwick and Oldbury. These replaced the FHA 8xx batch of SOS FEDDs on a virtual one-to-one basis. Foster Street Garage in Stourbridge had about half a dozen THA-registered D7s for the service to Wolverhampton via Kingswinford, and Wolverhampton Garage had the type for the intensive inter-urban routes to Birmingham, Stourbridge, Wombourne and Stafford. During their lives, Sutton Coldfield Garage had around twenty D7s. D7s were also allocated to Kidderminster Garage, while Lichfield, which was basically a single-deck garage, had a handful for routes operating to Stafford, who also had their own D7s for their town services. Redditch Garage received D7s for use on their busy services to Birmingham and Bromsgrove, while Tamworth also had a small number of D7s. Myton Road, Leamington Spa, had over twenty D7s operating on Leamington and Warwick town services as well for the route to Coventry. In less urbanised areas Evesham, Friar Street in Hereford and Malvern operated small numbers of D7s especially for their town routes.

In the East Midlands, Southgate Street in Leicester had nearly forty D7s while, in the mid-1950s, nearby Sandacre Street had all their wartime Guy Arab IIs replaced by the BMMO D7s. Wigston Garage had around fifty of the type to run the bus services operating southward from Leicester to Wigston, Oadby, Great Glen and Kibworth.

Coalville and Hinckley operated D7s, while the Markfield Garage, taken over on 16 March 1963 from Brown's Blue Coaches, had around fifteen D7s to replace the old, unused Brown's double-deckers until the garage closed on 30 June 1968. Nuneaton and Rugby also had a few D7s from the early 1960s.

Withdrawals began in April 1964 when 4111 was taken out of service and exported to Universal Studios, Hollywood, USA, for use as a studio tour bus. The second D7 to be sold was in March 1965 when 4110 also went to Universal. The D7s were not replaced by the BMMO D9s but rather by the 252 Daimler Fleetline CRG6LXs with Alexander bodywork delivered to Midland Red between 1966 and 1971. In 1966 eight of the THA batch were withdrawn, including 4163, which was written off after an accident in September of that year. A further fifty-five THA-registered D7s were taken out of service in 1967. In 1968, for the first time one of the XHA batch, 4530, was withdrawn. 1969 was a bad year, as forty D7s were withdrawn. In 1970 some seventy-two D7s were taken out of service, along with the first eleven from the final batch of fifty D7s. 1971 was second year of the mass-withdrawals, with 138 taken out of service. By the beginning of 1972, only twenty-five D7s were left, with five VHA-registered D7s going in this year along with five of the XHA group and the last fourteen of the remaining BHA vehicles. This left 4114 to soldier on at Dudley Garage until May 1973, where it frequently was used on the arduous 140 route from Birmingham to Dudley via Quinton, Blackheath and Rowley Regis.

A number of D7s from the THA batch were used as driver training vehicles (4082, 4098, 4116) or staff buses (4085, 4101–4103, 4120 and 4122) from around December 1967 until the autumn of 1970. From May 1972, eleven of the D7s saw additional use with BMMO as service vehicles. D7 4088 became a tree-lopper and mobile workshop in October 1968, replacing D5B 3787. Eleven buses were converted to towing lorries with remnants of the lower saloon kept for crew accommodation, and all were painted in all-over yellow service fleet colours. 4392 and 4531 passed to West Midlands PTE on 3 December 1973 and both were repainted in their blue-and-cream livery.

After the glamorous sale of 4110 and 4111 to Universal Studios in Hollywood, USA, only a few more prosaic sales for further service occurred. 4082, 4435 and 4759 went to Green's Coaches of Brierley Hill for service as a contractor's bus, surviving until 1977, while 4475 also appears to have been sold to a contractor. 4148 went to Hednesford Raceway and was used as a control vehicle. A number of D7s passed into preservation both as buses and as towing lorries. From the first batch, 4082 has been in long-term preservation in the Bromsgrove area, while 4110 is preserved in California in a blue-and-white livery. 4114, the aforementioned last D7 in service, is also complete and was last heard of stored in the Adlestrop area near Moreton-in-Marsh. ('Yes, I remember Adlestrop.') There are no VHA-registered D7s in preservation, although 4403, the first sixty-three-seater, was kept for some years as a preservation project. BaMMOT owns the well-restored 4482 (XHA 482), which entered service on 25 March 1956. In addition 4496 and 4750 are preserved as cut-down recovery vehicles at Wythall and recovery vehicles 4494, 4761 and 4767 are also privately owned.

4080, YHA 80

Charlton Street Garage, Wellington, was opened in September 1953, the same month that 4080, (THA 80), entered service. Although double-deckers were rarely allocated to the new garage, this D7 was chosen by the Omnibus Society for a tour around Shropshire – hence the 'SPECIAL' display in the destination blind. This BMMO D7 has a Metro-Cammell H32/26R body and was to last until November 1966. The clean four-bay lines of the bodywork suited the front bonnet design of the D7s and, although the body was a lightweight precursor to the Orion at around 7 tons 2 cwt, it was much more attractive, especially with its original yellow lining out. (D. R. Harvey collection)

4113, THA 113

Pulling away from a bus stop when working on the 825 service from Stafford to Lichfield via Rugeley on 30 August 1960 is 4113, (THA 113). The D7s had an improved version of the 8.028-litre BMMO K diesel engine, known as the BMMO 'KL' with the mounting of the engine and gearbox together in the chassis frame. This bus entered service on 1 January 1954 from Stafford Garage as a H32/26RD seater, but in 1955 was re-seated with the addition of five seats in the upper saloon, which was a boon to its carrying capacity, but made for somewhat cramped conditions. (G. Pattison)

4159, THA 159

After working on one of the city services, 4159, (THA 159), a 1954 BMMO D7 leaves Hereford Bus Station as it starts the short journey back to Hereford's bus garage. This bus was moved to work in Hereford in June 1962 and would spend the next seven years in the city. The Metro-Cammell bodywork on the D7 had fibre-glass front and rear domes, which rather spoilt the rest of the body, and frequently had a fibre finish. In the distant bus station is BMMO S14 4352, (UHA 352), the last of the 1956 batch of these lightweight single-deckers. (A. D. Broughall)

4359, VHA 359

The D7s were, for many years, the real workhorses of the Midland Red fleet. Although criticised for their rather parsimonious interior finish, they were mechanically very dependable and could be relied upon for either town services or long inter-urban routes. One of the second batch, 4359, (VHA 359), is working from Stafford towards Walsall and Dudley on the 865 route. It is beneath Walsall Corporation trolleybus wires at the Bloxwich terminus and is parked in front of one of that municipality's semi-low height Daimler CVG6s with a Willowbrook body, 840 (WDH 915), which were nicknamed 'jumping jacks' on account of their lively riding characteristics. (R. F. Mack)

4368, VHA 368

Although outwardly a standard D7, 4368, (VHA 368), had been fitted with an experimental SCG semi-automatic two-pedal control gearbox from 1957 until February 1969. Despite making the driver's life easier, the device was not a success. The bus was new in December 1954 and is working on the 252 route from Cape Hill via the Blue Gates in Smethwick to Dartmouth Square and then terminating at Carters Green with a journey time of just 18 minutes. 4368 is in Roebuck Lane, Smethwick, and is negotiating the narrow bridge over James Brindley's Birmingham Canal, which was opened in November 1769. Nearby is Thomas Telford's Birmingham Canal Navigations New Main Line, spanned by the magnificent Galton Bridge. This was named after local Quaker arms manufacturer Samuel Galton and opened in 1829, when it was the highest single span bridge in the world at 151 feet. Roebuck Lane is today only used as an access road to an industrial estate. (A. D. Broughall)

4410, VHA 410

The area around Burton was well covered by Midland Red. The 706 route went to the south west of the town to Linton. Metro-Cammell-bodied BMMO D7 4410, (VHA 410), stands in Burton Bus Station in the late 1950s. The bus had entered service in July 1955 and was one of the first to have the increased seating capacity of sixty-three. 4410 stayed at Swadlincote Garage for the next twelve years. (A. D. Packer)

4433, VHA 433

The 192 route took 2½ hours to complete the journey from Birmingham to Ludlow via Halesowen, Kidderminster and Cleobury Mortimer. Lying on the slopes of Titterstone Clee Hill about half way between Ludlow and Cleobury Mortimer on the A4117 road is the village of Cleehill. The village, which is home to the highest pub in Shropshire, stands at a height of 1296 feet above sea level and it is through this village that the 192 route operated. BMMO D7 4433, (VHA 433), heads westward towards Ludlow on the twisting and somewhat tortuous route between Bewdley and Cleobury Mortimer in about 1963. (D. R. Harvey)

4474, XHA 474

Loading up with passengers in the forecourt of Southgate Street Bus Garage in the summer of 1956 is one of that garage's allocation of BMMO D7s. An almost-new 4474, (XHA 474), is about to start on the long journey on the X68 service to Birmingham via Coventry. Delivered in February 1956, these buses provided a comfortable ride for long-distance passengers, even if the seat backs were rather low and failed to provide enough lumbar support, and the performance of the bus lacked the zip of an LD8. (A. D. Packer)

4509, XHA 509

Somewhat abandoned in the middle of Worcester Bus Station is Metro-Cammell-bodied BMMO D7 4509, (XHA 509). The bus, looking a little careworn, has arrived from Birmingham on the 144 service and will, in due course, move onwards on its journey to Malvern Wells. The bus is in the twilight of its career as it has Worcester Garage's destination blind fitted and was only operated by that garage between February 1968 and October 1970, when it was withdrawn. (D. R. Harvey collection)

4535, XHA 535

Wednesbury was only one of three towns in the West Midlands that the four municipal operators (Birmingham, Walsall, West Bromwich and Wolverhampton) and Midland Red actually served. 4535, (XHA 535), a Cradley Heath-garaged BMMO D7 delivered to that garage in October 1956, is in Wednesbury Bus Station when working on the 244 route to Cradley Heath. This was a service that crossed the Black Country from the traditional glass-blowing industrial area of the south west to the heavy industry and coal mining region of the northeast. (A. D. Broughall)

4723, 723 BHA

The juxtaposition of BMMO D7 4723, (723 BHA), parked outside the Cleveland Road Salvation Army Citadel, Wolverhampton, and the advertisement for Atkinsons Bitter on the side of the bus is perhaps a little inappropriate. The date is 21 March 1961 and, within a few years, much of this scene would have altered or disappeared. Atkinsons had already been taken over by M&B in 1959; the Wolverhampton Corporation trolleybus wires came down in March 1967; and this part of Cleveland Road is now a cul-de-sac. 4723 was the first of the final batch of fifty D7s to enter service in February 1957. Behind the MCCW-bodied double-decker is BMMO S14 4303, (UHA 303), working on the 893 service to Ironbridge and Shrewsbury. (G. Pattison)

4730, 730 BHA

Waiting at Stand No. 2 in Pool Meadow Bus Station, Coventry, is 4730, (730 BHA). This stand handled all the Midland Red services that served Leamington. This sixty-three-seater BMMO D7, new to Leamington Garage in February 1957, is working on the 517 route via Kenilworth in the early 1960. The conductor, with his highly polished shoes, sits on the railings, having left his ticket machine inside the bus but kept his money satchel with him. (D. R. Harvey collection)

4740, 740 BHA

Turning into St Peter's Hill in Grantham town centre with the 1869 Victorian Gothic Guildhall (designed by William Watkin with a huge bell tower), and the town's public library and art gallery behind it is 4740, (740 BHA), working on the long 662 service back to Leicester on 1 May 1965. The Metro-Cammell H37/26R-bodied BMMO D7 entered service in March 1957 and spent its entire life at Southgate Street Garage until it was withdrawn in February 1971. Just visible behind the D7 is a Lincolnshire Road Car Bristol Lodekka double-decker. (R. F. Mack)

4767, 767 BHA

Travelling away from Birmingham city centre along Hurst Street is 4767, (767 BHA), a BMMO D7 with a Metro-Cammell H37/26R body that entered service in September 1957. At this time in 1960, the bus has been spray painted and has red painted wings. It was allocated to Redditch Garage and is working back to its home town via Alvechurch on the 147 route and then onwards to Astwood Bank. After withdrawal in April 1972, this vehicle was converted into a recovery vehicle, initially for Nuneaton Garage, using the trade plate 290 HA until it was sold for preservation. (R. H. G. Simpson)

Double-Deckers Taken Over from Kemp & Shaw

The old established operator Kemp & Shaw of Mountsorrel ran its first bus services soon after the end of the First World War and, although taken over by Allen's Motor Services ion 1928, continued to work two main stage-carriage services between Leicester via Loughborough and Kegworth to Derby, and from Leicester to Birstall and on to Loughborough. The business, along with Allen's Motor Services, was sold to Midland Red on 30 July 1955. The company was then operated as a subsidiary until totally absorbed on 1 January 1959. Six double-decker Guy Arabs and two Leyland Titan PD2s, which had been numbered 24–27 and 30 and 31 in the Kemp & Shaw fleet, became 4838–4845 when absorbed into the Midland Red fleet. The missing two buses, 28–29, were Guy Arab III single-deckers with Barnard bodies and were 28 and 29 in the Kemp & Shaw fleet.

(24), 4838, DJF392

This was a Guy Arab II with a 16-foot 3-inch wheelbase, a Gardner 5LW 7.0-litre engine and a Northern Counties H30/26R, delivered in February 1946. The bus had a tall radiator and a sloping straight edge to the bottom of the windscreen, while the body was built to NCME's first post-war style. Although still based on the metal-framed wartime body, the design had rounded front and rear domes, half-drop opening windows and an outward curved tumblehome. It was withdrawn in January 1961 and then used as driver training vehicle at Sandacre Garage until April of that year.

(25), 4839, EBC882

This was a very similar Guy Arab II with a Gardner 5LW engine; it was built near to the end of Mark II production and delivered in November 1946. The NCME body was virtually the same as 24 but was equipped with sliding saloon ventilators. It was withdrawn in December 1960.

(26–27), 4840–4841, EJF668–669

These pair of Guy Arab IIIs with Gardner 5LW engines was delivered in November 1947. Differing by having a polished aluminium radiator, the Northern Counties H30/26R body was similar to that on 4839, though the bottom of the windscreen was straight in order to match the position of the top of the lower-mounted radiator. This pair of vehicles was taken out of service by Midland Red in December 1960 and January 1961 respectively.

(30) 4844, GRY763

Kemp & Shaw switched their allegiance to the Leyland Titan PD2 model and ordered GRY 763, which was delivered in July 1950. Numbered 30, it was a Leyland Titan PD2/1 with a Leyland 0.600 9.8-litre engine. It had a standard lowbridge Leyland body with a L27/26R layout. It was fitted with half-drop saloon window ventilators. Becoming Midland Red's 4844, it was quickly equipped with full Midland Red destination boxes. Despite being the only lowbridge double-decker vehicle ever operated by Midland Red, 4844 enjoyed a long life, not being withdrawn until June 1967.

(31) 4845, JBC989

Delivered to Kemp & Shaw in December 1952 as their fleet number 31, JBC 989 was a Leyland Titan PD2/12 with a Leyland H30/26R body. This bus was 27 feet long and 8 feet wide, built with the last style Leyland body design with recessed window pans. On passing to Midland Red it was renumbered 4845 and fitted with the standard Midland Red front destination box, while the rear platform was enclosed. As a result it appeared like an exposed radiator LD8 class. It was withdrawn in April 1967.

4838, DJF 392
Delivered in February 1946, a well-loaded 4838, (DJF 392), waits for its driver in St Margaret's Bus Station before leaving for Birstall. This Guy Arab II 5LW had a Northern Counties H30/26R body, built to their first post-war style but based on their metal-framed wartime bodies with rounded domes and four half-drop opening windows in each saloon. Formerly Kemp & Shaw's 24, it was taken into Midland Red stock on 1 January 1959 and withdrawn in January 1961, before briefly being used as a driver training vehicle at Sandacre Garage for three months. (D. R. Harvey collection)

4839, EBC 882
Turning into Burley's Way and following a razor-edged Triumph Mayflower is the former Kemp & Shaw 25 (EBC 882). Numbered 4839 in the Midland Red fleet, this Guy Arab II was delivered in November 1946 near to the end of that model's production. The NCME body was similar to the previous bus but had sliding saloon ventilators. Like all the former Kemp & Shaw vehicles taken over, it was operated from Sandacre Street Garage and was the first of their buses to be withdrawn in December 1960. (R. H. G. Simpson)

4841, EJF 669
A pair of Guy Arab IIIs with Gardner 5LW engines was delivered to Kemp & Shaw in November 1947. These buses had the new model's lower-mounted polished aluminium radiator. The Northern Counties H30/26R body had a horizontal bottom to the windscreen, which lined up with the top of the radiator. The second of these buses 4841, (EJF 669), is in St Margaret's Bus Station working on the Windmill Avenue service. This bus was withdrawn in January 1961. (A. J. Douglas)

4844, GRY 763

Kemp & Shaw ordered a Leyland Titan PD2/1 with a Leyland o.600 9.8-litre engine with a lowbridge Leyland L27/26R layout. GRY 763 was delivered in July 1950 and numbered 30 in their fleet. Becoming Midland Red's 4844, it was soon equipped with full Midland Red destination boxes. 4844 was the only lowbridge double-decker vehicle ever operated by Midland Red but, despite this, lasted in service until June 1967. It is working on the 617 route to the village of Thrussington located just off the A46 to the North East of Leicester. (D. R. Harvey collection)

4845, JBC 989

The last vehicle delivered to Kemp & Shaw was 31, (JBC 989). Arriving in December 1952, this was a Leyland Titan PD2/12 with a Leyland H30/26R body. This bus was 27 feet long and 8 feet wide built with the last style Leyland body design with recessed window pans. After being taken over by Midland Red, it became their 4845 and was quickly fitted with the standard Midland Red front destination box. 4845 is at Stand No. 4 in St Margaret's Bus Station in Leicester when working on the L40 local service to Birstall just off the A6. 4845 was withdrawn in April 1967. (A. D. Broughall)

The Introduction of the 30-Foot-Long BMMO D9

The post-war rear entrance half-cab D5, D5B and D7 models were, despite their concealed radiators, conservative in their chassis design when compared to Midland Red's post-war, trendsetting, underfloor-engined single-deckers. When the Construction and Use Legislation was increased to allow for 30-foot-long double-deckers in 1956, the preparatory work undertaken at Carlyle Road Works from 1951 was dusted down, and work re-commenced on a new double-decker design. It was at this point that Midland Red engineers and design staff began to produce something even more radical than the mainstream manufacturers.

4773 (773 FHA), the Prototype D9

In 1958, BMMO introduced the integral D9 model, which continued the BMMO philosophy of building mechanically advanced, fast, lightweight buses as cheaply as possible. This was in many ways a policy of great merit, providing maintenance levels could be kept up, but the D9 belonged to an era of even greater cost-cutting than the increasingly strapped-for-cash company could support.

The new prototype was numbered 4773 (773 FHA), and was a 30-foot-long half-cab double-decker of semi-integral design, using front and rear axle sub-frames to give extra rigidity. Like the advanced S14 single-decker of 1954, it had independent suspension on the front axle and, at first, disc brakes. It entered service from Sheepcote Street Garage in February 1959 on the 160 service from Birmingham to Coleshill.

The D9 has been nicknamed 'the Birmingham Routemaster' as, superficially, it had a lot of similarities to the AEC. Where it was different was that the front axle was set back, giving it a very short wheelbase for a conventional front-engined 30-foot-long double-decker of 17 feet 1½ inches, instead of the more normal wheelbase of about 18 feet 6 inches. The 10.5-litre BMMO KL engine was contained in a long, low, pleasantly proportioned bonnet, providing excellent forward vision and engine accessibility. The recessed windscreen was abandoned in favour of a neat flush fitting design. A very smooth curved profile, entirely free from any break in line, gave a sleek appearance. The large cab was reached by a door just in front of the set-back front axle. The driver also had a heater and demister in the cab.

The bus had an electrically controlled, hydraulically operated, direct-acting non-pre-selector four-speed gearbox, consisting of a combined fluid flywheel and centrifugal clutch that was made by Self-Changing Gears. This was operated by a five-gate gear lever to the left of the steering column. The fluid flywheel gave a smooth start from rest with the clutch providing a positive drive over 500 rpm, allowing for a fuel economy as good as a clutch and orthodox gearbox, at the expense of some transmission and gearbox noise given by full time flywheel. The rear axle was an underslung worm driven type. The bus also had power-assisted steering and variable-rate rubber suspension, with that at the front being independent while, following on from the S14 and S15 single-deckers, the early D9s had all-round servo-assisted disc brakes.

The Carlyle body for the prototype was built on Metal Sections all-steel frames that were ordered as early as April 1957. The bus had an H40/32RD seating split in a pleasant-looking if somewhat frugally finished body that did not do justice to the advanced specification of the underframe. The bus weighed 8 tons 2 cwt 3 qtrs. This lightweight body was clad in light alloy panels, while fibre-glass mouldings were used in the bonnet area, the curved front and rear corner panelling, the wings, and the front and rear domes and roof assembly. One unique distinguishing feature of 773 FHA was that it had one-piece lower saloon panels.

The interior colours were a rather sickly peony-and-white scheme, extensively incorporating the use of plastics like Formica or Darvic sheeting that eliminated the need for repainting. This prototype body behind the front bulkhead was essentially a 30-foot five-bay version of the previous BMMO D7, even having the same design of enclosed rear platform.

Production D9s

Construction of the first production batch of D9s, 4849–4942, got underway in 1959, again using Metal Section frames. These first production buses differed in a number of ways from 4773, with the moving of the 35 gallon fuel tank to the offside, a revised cab door, a taller, more stylish radiator grille, front plant on side lights and a simpler windscreen design. The bonnet was given a large chromed lifting handle while, in accordance with the latest regulations for 30-foot-long double-deckers, there was an offside emergency window in the lower saloon behind the driver's cab. The production vehicles had a polished aluminium rubbing strip all the way round the body that split these lower saloon panels, which made it both easier and cheaper to replace cheaper panels. Gears, steering and doors were also still affected by the hydraulic pressure deterioration. Because of heavy disc pad wear, the brake specification was soon changed to four-wheel hydraulically operated drum brakes, while the prototype's disc transmission handbrake was replaced on the production vehicles with a conventional handbrake. The production D9s weighed nominally 7 tons 18 cwt 2 qtrs, although this varied on individual buses by up to 2 hundredweight. The 30-foot-long by 8-foot-wide bus had a height of 14 feet 5 inches and, with a wheelbase of only 17 feet 1½ inches, had a tight turning circle of around 67 inches.

In January 1960, the first example to enter service, 4851 (851 KHA), started working from Bearwood Garage and, on 1 February 1960, 4852 and 4856 entered service from Birmingham's Sheepcote Street Garage; this eventually had the first few buses, including 4854 along with 4773, which moved to Sheepcote Street in February 1960.

First routes worked by the production D9s were the 160, 161 and 168 services to Coleshill. Around the same time Digbeth received the numerically first

D9 4849 (849 KHA), which was placed in service on the Birmingham and Solihull 154 route. By the end of the year, forty-nine production D9s had been delivered and replaced the last of the pre-war FEDDs. Deliveries of the first batch of D9s, 4849–4942, were completed by October 1961. In true Midland Red tradition the allocation of D9s was in penny numbers, generally to garages in Birmingham and the Black Country though Hinckley, Sandacre Street and Southgate Street in Leicester, also received early members of this first tranche of D9s.

The second batch was for 100 vehicles 4945–5044 (2945–3044 HA), with most of the first eight entering service in December 1961. The last seven buses, 5038–5044, arrived in February 1963 with one going to Southgate Street, two to Wigston, where they spent their entire lives, one to Bromsgrove Garage; two to Redditch; and the last one to Harts Hill. This strange piecemeal allocation of new buses was the norm for Midland Red, as buses were allocated more by need, so as one bus was cascaded elsewhere or withdrawn, the next suitable available bus would be sent to that garage. It was a system that worked but on paper looked messy!

The final production batch consisted of 150 buses and deliveries were somewhat protracted beginning in February 1963 and not being completed until November 1966. Numbered 5296–5445, their registrations (6296–6378 HA, AHA 379–394B, BHA 395–404C, EHA 405–445D) reflected the long period of manufacture and delivery. This final batch was fitted with an upgraded version of the BMMO KL 10.5-litre engine. Although compatible with the engines in the previous 195 D9s, in reality the newer engines were not placed in the earlier vehicles, as the spares for each were not themselves interchangeable.

BMC at Longbridge were recruiting large numbers of skilled, experienced body builders with wages far in excess to what Midland Red could ever hope to offer. This resulted in a large exodus of skilled body shop staff at this time to the local car industry, causing a loss of capacity at Carlyle Road Works with the result that, in 1965, D9 deliveries dropped sharply to only ten buses. At the same time Carlyle Works produced just under 100 of the new semi-automatic BMMO S17s 36-foot-long single-deckers to replace early post-war underfloor-engined single-deckers. In addition twenty of the twenty-nine CM6 coaches were also constructed in 1965. In order to complete the final D9 order, the last forty-five bodies, to be numbered 5401–5445, were completed by Willowbrook who had recently provided new bodies for Midland Red on Leyland Leopard chassis. The first of these out-shopped D9s began arriving at garages in December 1965, with the last five arriving eleven months later.

When these last five D9s, 5441–5445 (EHA 441–445D) had entered service in November 1966, 345 of the type had been built, a figure that was remarkably close to the 351 pre-war FEDDs, and the 350 of the preceding standard Midland Red double-decker, the D7. The 345 D9s were subjected to a wide range of both major and minor modifications during the production run. Most of these were brought in when the vehicles were new but a few were introduced retrospectively. As a result there were hardly any two D9s that were the same.

Around the end of the 1950s there was a trend to fit buses with external illuminated advertisements. After experiments with S14 4671, D9 bus 4872, delivered in July 1960, was equipped with an exterior illuminated panels on both sides. When working, the bus looked like something akin to the Blackpool Illuminations, but it was something of an electrical disaster. Due to the D9s having DC electrics, but the florescent tubes working on an AC system, a rectifier was required to convert the current for the advertisement panel to be lit up. If the dynamo failed to recharge the circuits it resulted in the batteries going flat.

In November 1960, 4887 was delivered with two separate destination screens mounted in their own rubbers, which became the standard arrangement for later buses. 4927 (927 KHA) was delivered in June 1961 with colour impregnated glass fibre panels. It was also fitted with extra polished around the cab, wheel arches and waistrail and had interior fluorescent lighting behind moulded jelly covers. Deemed more successful than the illuminated advertisement experiments, from bus 4988, all subsequent D9s had fluorescent saloon lighting. From bus 5023 (3023 HA), the distinguished maroon paintwork on the platform was replaced by a brighter red while, in 1963, 5319 and 5323 both had revised heating systems that were adopted as standard on all subsequent D9s. Seats varied over the production run; the first few D9s had moquette seats similar to those in the S15 dual-purpose bus, but most had separate rear back panels 'pads', introduced to facilitate easy damage repair.

The protruding mud wings were replaced by flush sided wheel arches with polished aluminium edgings on buses 5314/6–21 and, after 5326, this became standard. The simplicity of this design meant that the side panels were pre-fitted with a wheel arch, making repairs cheaper, but the unsupported curvature of the wheel arch was prone to cracking and many later buses had the flush arches reinforced with beading. The D9s with this feature were unofficially Mark II D9s.

As with the D7s, the single-skinned fibre-glass domes were also a problem. The rear domes had a tendency to crack around the top of the emergency window but it was the front dome and the Auster hopper ventilators in the front upper windows that were prone to failure. The front domes were attached to the main waist rail of the upper saloon but, because of the flexing of the bodywork, the dome itself would distort and crack, causing the opening ventilators to become misaligned and therefore difficult to open. This also distorted the window rubbers and this would crack the surrounding fibre glass. Various solutions were employed, such as fitting new domes with an added gusset above the front windows in order to strengthen the assembly or just by removing the hopper ventilators, giving the bus a somewhat denuded frontal appearance.

It was the reliance on only one hydraulic master tank, however, that was to prove the Achilles' heel of the D9. The system was used on BMMO-designed vehicles, which had a Constant Flow System (CFS) for operating the brakes. This consisted of a hydraulic servo over hydraulic brakes with the power coming from a Lucas hydraulic pump feeding the servo at a constant pressure of 1850 psi. The hydraulic brake circuit was set with the pump circuit drained of air. Both hydraulic circuits drew up fluid from a tank with one filler but two distinct compartments. The one part contained the fluid for the brake circuit proper and, when that was full, the fluid spilled over through a hole in the neck into an outer tank, which acted as the reservoir for the pump circuit. If not filled correctly, air got into the servo system, rendering the brakes poor. The hydraulic circuit was driven off the prop shaft, which at low speed contributed to the lack of brakes, especially in slow traffic. The instant the driver lifted the pedal, the servo assistance was lost and the brakes began to fade. Drivers tended to blame this on poor maintenance while engineers blamed the drivers!

When new they were painted in all-over red with gold and black fleet names and numbers. In 1970 this style was replaced by an underlined lower case fleet name and the gold replaced by yellow, but, after the corporate livery of the National Bus Company was set up in 1974, the buses were repainted in poppy red with grey wheels and the NBC logo and the fleet name in white. Additionally six D9s – 5311, 5319, 5412, 5413, 5415 and 5422 – were given all-over advertisements, usually for about twelve months, before returning to the standard fleet livery.

The first withdrawals of the 345 D9s occurred in January 1969, when the nearly seven-year-old 5298 was destroyed by fire. In 1971, 4861, 4864, 4878 and 5343 were withdrawn due to accident damage while, in October, 5391 went due to fire damage. The first proper withdrawals began in 1972 when the prototype, 4773, was withdrawn in June while another twenty-eight production buses went, with 4867 going first. In 1973, a total of fifty-eight D9s were withdrawn, of which sixteen were from the KHA batch and forty-two were from the second 100 with reverse HA registrations.

If that wasn't enough, ninety D9s were compulsorily transferred to the West Midland PTE on 3 December 1973, of which thirty were from the first batch with reverse KHA registrations, twenty-two from the second batch and the remaining thirty-eight being from the D9s registered between 1963 and 1966. Withdrawals of the WMPTE D9s began as early as April 1974, when three buses were withdrawn and, by the end of that year, a further eight had gone. None of these D9s received the blue-and-cream livery of WMPTE. Regarding the D9 liveries used by West Midlands, initially many of the buses retained their red liveries and were fitted with red-ground vinyl fleet names and legal lettering. In 1975, eleven more, still in their Midland Red colours, had been taken out of service. All other D9s were repainted in the West Midlands Oxford blue-and-cream livery, which suited them very well. Unlike Midland Red's general numerical withdrawal of D9s, WM D9 withdrawals were based purely on the vehicle's condition, irrespective of its age. In 1976, West Midlands withdrew another thirty-three D9s including 4849, the first production bus. Of these, Oldbury Garage's allocation of around twenty D9s, used to work the intensive 87 service, were replaced by the first thirty of the splendid Alexander-bodied Volvo Ailsa B55s. This left the final thirty going during 1977, of which the last five were 5322, 5342, 5349, 5422 and 5444, which went in October 1977, with the now preserved 5342 becoming the last D9 in service, operating a farewell enthusiasts' tour. The disposals of the WMPTE D9s were to Birds of Stratford; Booth and Rollinson, both of Rotherham; PVS of Barnsley; and Paul Sykes of Blackerhill. 5353 was sold to Telson Metals in Knights Road, Birmingham, who seemed to buy one bus for breaking once a decade.

Meanwhile Midland Red's withdrawal programme continued apace. In 1974, forty-one D9s were withdrawn, while in 1975 another thirty-two were taken out of service. In 1976, thirty-seven buses, including the last three, 4881, 4885 and 4899 were withdrawn from the first batch, as well as 4986 and 4988 from the second 100.

The final 'mass' withdrawals were in 1977 when thirty-five D9s were made redundant, leaving just five buses to be taken out of service during 1978. This left thirteen D9s, all of which were allocated to Southgate Street in Leicester. Although these survivors were not due to be phased out until February 1980, their withdrawal occurred on New Year's Eve 1979. During their last fortnight of service, the weather deteriorated, with some appalling snow storms making the route to Scraptoft a real struggle, but the last buses went out working as hard as they had usually done in the past. The last one into the garage was 5314, but this was done with little ceremony to commemorate the final demise of the D9s in Midland Red service. 5399 was kept licensed until March 1980, but was retained and restored by the Midland Red Omnibus and operated on special services from Cannock garage for two years from July 1982.

Disposals of Midland Red D9s for scrap were to Hudley of Bilston, Longbridge Engineering of Marlbrook, Taylor of Stafford, Dowen of Bloxwich and Ensign of Grays, who sold most of them for further use. Later withdrawals were sold to Paul Sykes, who was the only dealer to break up D9s from both Midland Red and West Midlands PTE. In 1974, the Greys-based dealer, Ensign, sold a total of twenty-one buses to other operators, including the eleven leased to Lesney Products, makers of Matchbox Toys, for staff transport between their two factories in Hackney and Rochford. The buses were painted in the Matchbox Toy box colours of deep blue with a yellow band. Ensign also sold six D9s in September 1974 to Thomas Morris of Pencoed near Bridgend. They were operated on a school contract to Cowbridge in a livery of medium blue with white relief until the end of the summer term of 1976.

The first real attempt to use open-top tour buses for sightseeing around London was instigated by the pioneer bus preservationist Prince J. Marshall as the Obsolete Fleet. Between 1974 and 1980 the company purchased ten D9s, of which seven were converted to open top condition by LPC Coachworks of Hounslow. These were numbered OM1-7, while two others, numbered BM 8 and 9, were left as built, for use during inclement weather. The Obsolete buses were painted in London Transport Red with white LT roundels and began operating from Stockwell garage on 26 April 1975. In 1981 Prince Marshall died and, by the end of 1982, London Transport closed the operation and instigated their own open-top tours using converted short-length AEC Routemasters.

Fortunately, there are at least twelve D9s that are preserved, of which several are fully restored and are regularly operated. The 4773 (773 FHA) prototype is preserved, while three D9s – 4871 (871 KHA), in WMPTE livery; 5016 (3016 HA), as Obsolete Fleet OM5 in open-top condition; and fully operational 5399 (BHA 399C) – are all at BaMMOT, Wythall. 5035 (3035 HA) is at the Aldridge Museum in open-top condition along with Richard Grey's fully restored 5370 (6370 HA). 5342 (6342 HA) is operated by the Black Country Living Museum, Dudley. Unrestored 5301 (6301 HA) is still extant with Black Country Tours, Netherton, in open-top condition and 5314 (6314 HA), the last one in service at Leicester, is also unrestored. 5415 (EHA 415D) is operated by Big Red Bus, Wirral, and 5424 (EHA 424D) by Roger Burdett of Long Eaton. In addition, there is 4903 (903 KHA) in open-top condition in Zwickau, Germany.

The D9 could be found across the whole of Midland Red's huge operating area. These big seventy-two-seaters were at home on the intensive services in Birmingham and Black Country and on the heavily subscribed services from Leicester. They were used extensively on town routes in places as diverse as Worcester, Stafford, Leamington, Shrewsbury and Hereford, and were comfortable on long cross-country services such as Birmingham–Leicester via Coventry, Shrewsbury–Hereford via Ludlow and Leominster, and routes such as Birmingham–Malvern via Worcester, routes to Coventry from Leamington Spa, via Warwick and those from Birmingham to Sutton Coldfield, Tamworth, Coleshill and Nuneaton. Yet the D9 was equally at home just pootling around village services in rural Warwickshire, Worcestershire and Shropshire. The D9 continued the BMMO philosophy of building mechanically advanced, fast, lightweight buses as cheaply as possible. This was in many ways a policy of great merit, providing maintenance levels could be kept up, but the D9 belonged to an era of even greater cost-cutting than the increasingly strapped-for-cash company could support.

The D9 was a very advanced bus, possibly even too advanced for its own good. Yet 345 of them were built and some had long lives. When a D9 was perfectly maintained and was in good order, it was undoubtedly a bus that was a delight to drive with an abundance of power and able to effortlessly carry a full load. The trouble was that the D9 had too many inherent faults caused by the Lockheed hydraulic system, which affected the brakes, steering and gears and even the platform doors, while parts of the body, namely the structures in the upper saloon, were far too lightweight. The length of their operating lives of up to fifteen years was remarkably good, suggesting that the underlying engineering concept of the D9 was basically sound, but attention to detail and maintenance was their Achilles' heel.

4773, 773 FHA
The prototype BMMO D9 was 4773, (773 FHA), whose Carlyle-built H40/32R body, constructed using Metal Section framework made in Oldbury, looked like a lengthened D7 with one extra bay, an effect enhanced by the full length lower saloon panels and the lack of chrome body trim. The bus is in Moor Street at its Birmingham city centre terminus in about 1960. It is standing in front of Edwardian-built former Great Western Railway's Moor Street station and will soon depart to Solihull by way of Stratford Road through Hall Green and Shirley. (P. Yeomans)

4849, 849 KHA

Numerically the first production BMMO D9 was 4849, (849 KHA). This bus entered service in February 1960 as the second of these buses to be delivered after 4851 went on the road in the previous month. Its Carlyle H40/32RD body was ideal for routes such as the 154 service, where high loadings on such busy services suddenly became manageable. It is passing Digbeth Garage in Digbeth as it travels into Birmingham from Solihull with the cupola-topped Digbeth Civic Hall behind the bus. Following the bus is a two-tone Ford Zodiac I EOTTA six-cylinder saloon. (D. R. Harvey collection)

4875, 875 KHA

Showing off its illuminated advertisement, appropriately exclaiming about the possible £500,000 win on Littlewoods Football Pools, BMMO D9 4875, (875 KHA), stands in New Street in front of 5279, (5279 HA), one of the 1963 DD11 Alexander-bodied rear-engined Daimler Fleetline CRG6LXs, a type that would eventually kill off the front-engined D9 double-decker. 4875 is working on the 160 route to Kingshurst in 1963 and is standing in front of the late 1930s Littlewoods Building, part of the same Liverpool-based company who were advertising a different product on the side of the bus. (A. D. Broughall)

4898, 898 KHA
Travelling through Hereford city centre on the H4 town service is 4898, (898 KHA), a BMMO D9 with a Carlyle H40/32R body that had entered service in January 1961. It was fitted with an offside illuminated advertisement panel soon after it moved to Hereford Garage in October 1961. When new these 30-foot-long, seventy-two-seaters must have been a revelation as they enabled journey times to be cut due their large and powerful BMMO 10.45-litre engines, they were manoeuvrable and had easy driving characteristics. Problems would emerge later! (G. Pattison)

4927, 927 KHA
Possibly the easiest BMMO D9 to identify was 4927, (927 KHA). The body was built with experimental impregnated fibre-glass panels with a considerable amount of extra polished aluminium added to its Carlyle H40/32R body. It has just entered Harborne Road, Birmingham, with the busy Five Ways junction behind it. The bus is working on the 130 service to Halesowen and Stourbridge and is pulling into a temporary Midland Red bus stop. Behind the bus is Philip Chatwin's classically designed Portland stone-faced Lloyds Bank opened in 1909 and the Victorian Five Ways Clock, erected to commemorate Birmingham's first coroner, Dr John Birt Davies. (A. D. Broughall)

4953, 2953 HA

Turning out of Edgbaston Street, having just left the subterranean Bull Ring bus station in Birmingham, is 4953, (2953 HA). This BMMO D9 entered service on January 1962 and passed to WMPTE on 3 December 1973 when based at Dudley Garage. It survived with the PTE until July 1976 and is operating on the 125 service to Dudley and Wolverhampton in about 1974, wearing the Oxford blue-and-cream livery of West Midlands PTE. It is being followed by an ex-BCT Park Royal-bodied two-doored Daimler Fleetline. (D. R. Harvey collection)

4959, 2959 HA

4959, (2959 HA), by now numbered OM3 in Prince Marshall's Obsolete Fleet and converted to an open-top bus for tourist work around the sights of London, comes out of Whitehall and into Trafalgar Square, in the centre of the Birmingham tramway network. The open-top conversion job was very neat, and retained the front windows and the remnants of the original D9 type upper saloon windows. The bus is surrounded by Austin FXB 4 taxi cabs working their way around central London and Westminster. OM3s' conversion to open top was undertaken in February 1975 by LPC Coachworks Limited of Hounslow and, in turn, these former Midland Red vehicles would be replaced by the converted open-top Routemaster buses. (MB Transport)

4969, 2969 HA

4969, (2969 HA), is sporting an offside illuminated advertisement, somewhat nepotistically for Midland Red's own recently introduced non-stop M1 Motorway Express service between Birmingham, Coventry and London. This Carlyle-bodied D9 entered service in March 1962 from Cradley Heath Garage and is being used on the 137 route to Gornal Wood via Brierley Hill. The bus is standing in Stephenson Street with the Austin Princess limousine parked behind it on the forecourt of New Street Station and beneath the shadow of the soon-to-be demolished Queen's Hotel. (D. R. Harvey collection)

5014, 3014 HA

On 2 April 1977 a British Railways DMU failed to stop at the Stourbridge Town Station and careered to a halt that left it balanced over Foster Street, opposite the bus garage. A crowd have come to watch the aftermath of the runaway train as one of the BMMO D9s taken over by West Midlands PTE leaves the forecourt of Stourbridge Garage when starting the journey back to Dudley on the 246 route. 5014, (5014 HA), had been at Sutton Coldfield Garage until it was taken over by the PTE on 3 December 1973, whereupon it was sent to Dudley Garage and spent its declining years in the Black Country. (D. R. Harvey collection)

5028, 3028 HA

Working on the X35 service towards Hereford, 5028, 3028 HA, a BMMO D9 dating from January 1963 and fitted with an illuminated advertisement panel, had just passed the Green Dragon public house in Ludlow Road at the edge of Little Stretton. The bus is travelling south towards the A49 and on towards Hereford, having left behind Church Stretton, though it appears to a lonely turn as the driver and conductor appear to be the only occupants of the double-decker. (D. R. Harvey collection)

5305, 6305 HA

The family resemblance between the central parts of the BMMO D9 bodywork built at Carlyle Road Works on Metal Section framework on 5305, (6305 HA), and the Metro-Cammell body on a THA-registered BMMO D7 is most noticeable. Both buses are in Shrewsbury Bus Station on 20 June 1964. The D9, which spent its entire service life from March 1963 to December 1974 working from Shrewsbury Garage, is working on the S5 service to Weeping Cross while the D7 is off to Ragloth Gardens. (A. D. Packer)

5314, 6314 HA

By now painted in NBC poppy red, the last D9s owned by Midland Red were operated from Southgate Street and used on the 93 route to Scraptoft and New Parks as operated by 5314, (6314 HA), on 20 December 1979, as well as services to Wigston and Thurmaston. The D9s were due to be taken off the road earlier, but the deliveries of new buses were delayed and the last six D9s soldiered on to New Year's Eve in the most appalling weather. On several days bus services in Leicester were curtailed but, despite some starting issues due to the freezing conditions, the D9s kept going. (D. R. Harvey collection)

5340, 6340 HA

A pair of BMMO D9s with Carlyle H40/32R bodies travel down Hill Street in 1974 soon after their absorption into the West Midlands PTE fleet. They have yet to be repainted and are still in the BMMO red livery with WM fablon stickers. 5340, (6340 HA), entered service in August 1963 and is about to turn into Station Street on its way into the Bull Ring Bus Station when working in from Wolverhampton on the 125 route. Following it is 5368, (6368 HA), dating from January 1964, revealing slowing down of the production of barely thirty new double-decker D9s at Carlyle Road Works. (D. R. Harvey collection)

5342, 5342 HA

This is what harmonious bus preservation is all about! BMMO D9 5342, (5342 HA), owned by the Black Country Living Museum's Transport Group in Dudley, stands in a bus layby in Alcester Road South, Hollywood, on 14 October 2007. It is parked behind the author's former Birmingham City Transport 2489, (JOJ 489), a Crossley-bodied Crossley dating from July 1950, when both buses are operating on a preserved bus service on behalf of the Wythall Bus Museum. The Carlyle H40/32RD bodied 5342 was new to Stourbridge Garage in September 1963 and passed to WMPTE on 3 December 1973, being withdrawn in October 1977. (D. R. Harvey)

5368, 6368 HA

Looking very smart in its newly acquired Oxford blue-and-cream West Midland PTE livery is 5368, (6368 HA). It is in Dudley Street when working on the 130 route from Stourbridge via Halesowen and Bearwood, and is passing the top entrance into Birmingham's Bull Ring bus station. The bus looks strangely denuded as it has lost its opening upper saloon front ventilators due to the need to make the fibre-glass front dome more rigid and less prone to cracking. (D. R. Harvey)

5419, EHA 419D

Having just arrived in Pool Meadow Bus Station in Coventry is 5419, (EHA 419D), one of the later D9s with bodywork completed by Willowbrook. Delivered in March 1966 to Digbeth Garage, it was only fourteen months old when it was in company with Alexander-bodied Daimler Fleetline CR6LX 5996, (GHA 396D). The D9 was an excellent bus for long journeys such as this, the 159 route from Birmingham to Coventry, a route that served the then Elmdon Airport as well as Stonebridge and Meriden. This particular vehicle would pass to WMPTE and remain in use with them until November 1976. (J. S. Cockshott)

5436, EHA 436D

Parked in front of Willowbrook's factory in Loughborough on 13 June 1966 is the just-completed 5436, (EHA 436D), which has yet to be fitted with any destination blinds. Alongside is 5442, (EHA 442D), having arrived with its body just a completed frame. The fibre-glass roof, and front and rear domes have been put in place but require completion. The rest of the bus lacks all of its panelling but all the stress panels are in place. (A. A. Turner)

The D10s

At a very early stage of D9 production, the design of two totally new underfloor-engined double-deckers was put in hand. These were given the designation D10 and were very advanced, thoughtful designs that briefly put Midland Red at the forefront of British double-decker development. The Midland Red solution to locating the engine underfloor was comparatively simple and ingenious. The deepest part of any horizontal engine is the flywheel housing, which normally on a single-decker lies at the centre of the vehicle with the cylinder heads and all the auxiliaries facing the nearside of the chassis. On the D10, the horizontal BMMO 10.5-litre KL engine was fitted inside the 16-foot 9-inch wheelbase and turned round, so that the flywheel was on the nearside and the cylinder heads faced towards the centre-line of the bus. This enabled the engine being set just above the legal minimum set by 1961 legislation of 10-inch ground clearance. Overcoming all these design problems was quite remarkable, ensuring that the gangway floor was now only 2 feet 3¼ inches above ground height, enabling the body to have a single entrance step on to the platform, which was only 14½ inches from the ground. Once through the electrically operated front doors, there was a flat floor throughout the length of the lower saloon, though the forward-facing seats on the near-side were raised about 2½ inches in order to clear the engine. In the lower saloon there were thirty-five seats, of which eighteen faced forward within the wheelbase, as well as the five seats across the rear of the saloon. The overall height of the D10 was 14 feet 4½ inches, including a lower saloon height of 5 feet 11¼ inches and an upper saloon height of 5 feet 9¼ inches. By employing lightweight moulded glass-fibre and standard D9 components within the D10's Metal Sections body frame, the unladen weight of the first D10 was kept down to 8 tons 10½ cwt, or nearly half a ton less than a contemporary Leyland Atlantean.

The Metal Sections frames ordered in May 1959 used many D9 components, but the bodies were built specifically for the pair of D10s numbered 4943 (943 KHA) and 4944 (1944 HA).

The driver sat in a cab not dissimilar to the contemporary S17 single-deckers, though the steering wheel was at a very flat, almost trolleybus-like angle. There was no external driver's door, so the cab was accessed by a low half-door on the platform opposite the entrance. The D10 had an electrically operated CAV semi-automatic four-speed electro-hydraulic-controlled semi-automatic gearbox mounted on the nearside dash, below the recessed windscreen rather than on the steering column; this made the reach for some drivers a little awkward when changing gears. The bus had hydro-steer power steering operating the D9 type Marles cam and roller steering, Girling front disc brakes and a Metalastic rubber suspension system, which had been standard BMMO practice since the introduction of the S14s. The gearbox was mounted directly onto the engine, with the fluid coupling and centrifugal clutch between the two. A transfer box was fitted to get the drive to the offset D9-style differential.

Midland Red considered that the two D10s were just two more underfloor-engined buses in a large fleet of underfloor-engined single-deckers. As a result, maintenance and repairs on the two D10s could be undertaken over a pit in just the same way that had been evolved by the company since it pioneered the type some fifteen years earlier with the first S6 single-deckers. The basic layout of 4943, the first D10, was H43/35F. It was shown to the press on 2 September 1960, but did not enter revenue service until 10 January 1961 from Digbeth Garage, where it was used on the 159 Birmingham–Coventry service. The prototype remained on its own until it was joined in April by the second D10, 4944, which entered service on the 160 service to Kingshurst in the following month. Not for the first time in the history of BMMO, this second bus showed Midland Red's somewhat idiosyncratic style and individuality of thought. It had an H37/28D layout with two sets of electrically operated doors – one a normal width front entrance and the second a narrow single-width rear exit served with a second rear staircase. The new bus was designated D10 Mark II and, with all the extra equipment of the extra rear staircase and second rear door, this second D10 weighed 8 tons 14¼ cwt.

The aim of Midland Red was to compare the two D10s in day-to-day operation, but it quickly became obvious that the Mark II was not proving as popular, especially with the conductors. It took longer to load and unload and this resulted, in November 1962, to the D10 Mark II being rebuilt to H43/43F. The loss of one seat compared to 4943 was due to the lower saloon emergency exit door being placed centrally in the back of the bus. This gave the bus a 'three-windowed-look' reminiscent of pre-war Midland Red FEDD double-deckers. 4943 had its lower saloon emergency exit conventionally placed on the offside with two windows and a five-seater bench seat at the back of the bus.

After over a year in service, both D10s were taken away from Digbeth and briefly allocated to Harts Hill Garage, being used on the 246 route between Dudley, Brierley Hill, Amblecote and Stourbridge. This extremely busy service was perhaps a 'little too much too soon' and, by 1963, both D10s had gone to Stafford Garage for use on the town services, on the 825 to Rugeley and Lichfield and, occasionally, on the 196 Stafford–Wolverhampton–Birmingham service. The two D10s remained at Stafford Garage until their withdrawal. 4943 was taken out of service in 1972 and was immediately taken back to Carlyle Road Works, where it was stored before being purchased by Brian Kelsall for preservation. The Mark II bus, 4944, survived until the next year, when it was sold to Taylors, a Stafford-based scrap merchant. The owners of 4943 stripped the Mark II bus for spares before the latter was broken up. The D10 remained in private hands until it was purchased for continued preservation by the Birmingham & Midland Motor Omnibus Trust at Wythall. A look at 4943 today is testimony enough to an unrealised potential that, forty years later, is still worthy of further development.

The D10's imaginative design used updated underfloor engine ideas within an existing advanced double-decker and was a great achievement, but was not developed as it was a child of an elderly and nearly bankrupt parent. When the two buses entered service, the D9 was in production and was proving to be everything that the company required. Had Midland Red been able to justify the cost of development, the

D10 might have gone into production and the last 150 D9s could have emerged as the production batch of D10s. As late as the spring of 1962, the shareholders' meeting was told that the new underfloor double-decker would go into production. Nevertheless, development costs were becoming prohibitive and the order for the cheaper option of fifty 'off-the-peg' Alexander-bodied Daimler Fleetlines was placed.

4943, 943 KHA

The concept of an underfloor-engined double-decker was fraught with problems concerning ground clearance, stability, sufficient saloon headroom and intrusions into the lower saloon floor. The D10 achieved all these criteria with a headroom of 5 feet 11¼ inches in the lower deck and 5 feet 9¼ inches upstairs within an overall vehicle height of 14 feet 4½ inches. Additionally it had the driver alongside the front entrance, thereby making the bus suitable for conversion to driver-only operation. Working on the S84 Stafford town service to the village of Doxey, to the northwest of the town, 4943, (943 KHA), is parked in the town centre and its Carlyle H45/35F body is a neat-looking cross between a D9 and a shortened S17. (D. R. Harvey collection)

4943, 943 KHA

Working on the 245 route from Dudley to Brierley Hill and Stourbridge and passing the Wagon & Horses Public House is 4943, (943 KHA), the first BMMO D10. Operating with the front doors open, at first sight this revolutionary underfloor vehicle looked like any other bus, except for the slightly higher than normal lower saloon's bottom window level. Launched to the press on 2 September 1960, 4943 was allocated to Hart's Hill Garage from May 1961 until April 1964, and spent much of its time operating on the extremely busy 245 service. (C. W. Routh)

4944, 1944 HA
Parked in the Birmingham Street section of Dudley Bus Station is 4944, (1944 HA), in the
summer of 1961 in its original condition. It is waiting to take up service on the 245 route to
Stourbridge. This was the second prototype BMMO D10 and was designated the Mark II. It had
a Carlyle H37/28D body with twin staircases and twin doors, and had entered service in May
1961. In this form it was considered to be unsuccessful and was rebuilt to a single door H43/34F
layout with rear staircase removed in November 1962. (A. D. Broughall)

4944, 1944 HA
A rare duty on the 140 route shows 4944, (1944 HA), in Dudley Bus Station after it had been
rebuilt to a H43/34F layout. The BMMO D10 Mark II had the emergency door positioned at the
rear of the bodywork, which harked back to the designs of the SOS FEDD era of the 1930s. The
lack of money, foresight and enthusiasm for the development of the D10 concept meant that a
projected order for fifty buses was not pursued and the D9, still advanced though comparatively
old fashioned, continued in production until 1966. (L. Mason)

The Midland Red Fleetline Era, DD11, 12, and 13

By the time the last of the second batch of BMMO D9s, 5044, was delivered in February 1963, the first double-decker to have a chassis bought from an 'outside' manufacturer since the LD8s was approaching completion at a coach-building factory in Falkirk. The chassis type was the rear-engined Daimler Fleetline CRG6LX and, between the arrival of the first bus, 5245 in March 1963 and 6293 in January 1971, 303 Alexander-bodied Fleetlines had entered service with Midland Red.

The reason for purchasing the initial batch of fifty Daimler buses was always stated by the BMMO management as being that they could not produce enough homemade BMMO D9s to cover the withdrawal of the early post-war double-deck fleet. The real reason might be not that straightforward as, by 1962, the wages being offered by BMC at 'The Austin' at Longbridge in Birmingham took many coachbuilders away from Carlyle Road. The policy of Midland Red's concentration on the construction of 36-foot-long BMMO S16 and S17 single-deckers slowed down the production of D9s, but there was the suspicion that there was else something wrong. The two D10s were in service and showing promise, although they were not without teething problems and, with 195 D9s on the road, superficially all would seem to be well. Yet, despite production costs rising, it was not just price that would cause Midland Red to look elsewhere for their next generation of double-deckers.

In 1962 the first large orders began to be placed for the Daimler Fleetline. After orders from Nottingham City Transport for eighteen and Manchester for twenty, Belfast City Transport ordered eighty-eight buses with MH Cars bodies, while nearby Birmingham City Transport were about to place a huge order for 300 Daimler Fleetlines with the body contract being split between Metro-Cammell and Park Royal. The advantage of having a rear-engined, front entrance bus with a door operated by the driver was an attractive proposition with the future prospect of One Man Operation.

Without trialling a demonstrator Midland Red placed an order with Daimler with chassis numbers in a block from 60191 to 60240, although the Midland Red fleet numbers were not in order. Even more surprisingly, the body contract was placed with Walter Alexander of Falkirk, who was barely known south of the border at this time for supplying double-deck bodies.

The fifty buses were numbered 5245–5294 (5245–5294 HA) and, when delivered, looked extremely smart. The new vehicles were given the Midland Red designation of DD11 buses, and any mention of them having chassis manufactured by Daimler was not displayed on the vehicles. As if to throw the unwary passengers off the scent of the chassis' origin, on the front panel below the windscreen was a large chromed BMMO badge! The Fleetlines were fitted with Gardner 6LX 10.45-litre engines, which was coupled to an SCG semi-automatic gearbox with two-pedal control.

The bodywork was derived from the design standardised by Glasgow Corporation. Designated the A type by Alexander, the body had an H44/33F layout, designed to be converted to OMO operation as soon as legislation was approved. These conversions eventually began in 1966, though it was not until 1968 that the buses were operated as driver-only vehicles. The Alexander bodies had a large V-shaped two-piece windscreen and a shaped moulding below the windscreen with both outer thirds being recessed and containing the headlights and the nearside spotlight. This attractive style of front not only got rid of the square box body look that was found on many early rear-engined chassis, but deflected the air flow around the bus to prevent the lower saloon windows from getting covered in road dirt. Turbulence was created towards the rear of the vehicle and thereby improved the cooling of the side-mounted radiator in the offside of the engine bustle. The front upper saloon windows, which were large and slightly angled, were coupled to the pair of raked opening hopper ventilators and gave the bodies a slightly worried look, echoing the same glum expression of the early post-war Brush-bodied buses. The DD11s were also fitted with illuminated advertisement panels, though many of these were never used. From the rear, the squared rear dome was fitted with a twin-window emergency exit. All the DD11s, which weighed exactly 8½ tons, arrived in an all-over unrelieved red livery with gold 'MIDLAND' lettering. The buses were not as comfortable as their earlier brethren, having rather hard seating with low backs, while the interiors were distinctly lacking in hand rails. Further to their design weakness, the interiors were painted with sickly pink ceilings and light beige side panels, which induced a feeling of nausea even for those passengers who did not suffer from travel sickness.

They arrived in considerable numbers, with nineteen entering service during March 1963 and all fifty in service by June, thus stealing a march on BCT, whose first Daimler Fleetlines were only just entering service. The DD11s were not specifically bought to replace any particular type of older double-deckers in the fleet. Initial allocations of the DD11s were predictably in the West Midlands, whose seven garages had thirty-one, while the three Leicester area garages had nineteen.

5261 was fitted with a transversely mounted BMMO 10.5-litre KL engine when it was new in April 1963, which it retained until it was replaced by a Gardner 6LX engine in September 1969. Quite a number of the class had their opening front ventilators in the upper saloon replaced by plain glass.

Four of the fifty – 5260, 5274, 5289 and 5290 – were all prematurely withdrawn between 1970 and 1972, having caught fire, while another twenty-one – 5246–7/51–3/55–6/9/61/68/70/2/5/7/9–80/3/6–8 and 5291 – were transferred to West Midlands PTE on 3 December 1973. All were painted in West Midland's livery of Oxford blue and cream, with a few receiving a thin blue line at upper saloon floor level, indicating the work of Walsall Works. Of these twenty-one buses 5246 was also a victim of fire damage and was the first WMPTE withdrawal in August 1975. The first normal PTE withdrawals began in October 1977 with 5277, while the rest were steadily taken out of service over the next two years, leaving the final two, 5252 and 5255, to become the last PTE withdrawals in

October and December 1980. Of those which remained with Midland Red, these were re-designated D11 in 1974. Sixteen went to City of Oxford Motor Services mainly in December 1976 and were given fleet numbers 908–923. Potteries Motor Traction also bought five as their 2001–2005, the last going in January 1980.

Having made the decision around the end of 1965 not to build any further 'in-house' BMMO D9s and to farm out the completion of the final forty-five D9 body frames, there was a pressing need to purchase a substantial number of new double-deckers. Midland Red returned to Daimler and ordered another 149 chassis, with bodywork again supplied by Alexander. Designated DD12, the new buses were numbered 5992–6140 but, as their protracted delivery was between August 1966 and January 1968, their registrations covered three registration suffix letters. GHA 392D–440D were all delivered by January 1967; JHA 42E–91E arrived between April and July 1967; while the last forty nine, registered LHA 592F–640F, began entering service in November 1967. All were in service by January 1968.

The chassis numbers of the DD12s were from 61543 to 61691, only this time the fleet, registration and Alexander body numbers were in strict sequential order. As Daimler issued chassis numbers on a block basis on receipt of the contract being signed, the protracted delivery of these buses could have only been due to either delays at Alexander, which seems improbable as the last forty-nine were delivered in three months, or, more likely, that the cash-strapped Midland Red were spreading the financial burden over a longer period. The DD12s were virtually the same as the DD11s except that the upper saloon front windows in the Alexander bodywork were devoid of the 'worried-looking' opening front ventilators. All of the 5992–6140 batch were converted to OMO from 1969 onwards.

The initial allocations of the DD12 were to the West Midlands, with the Birmingham and Black Country garages having a total of twenty-three, while Sutton Coldfield Garage had seven and neighbouring Tamworth had four for the busy commuter services into Birmingham. To the south west of Midland Red's operating area, Kidderminster received seven and Redditch eight, while four DD12s were delivered to Bromsgrove Garage. The two largest numbers of these second-generation Fleetlines were those at Worcester, which got fifteen new DD12s, and Leamington Garage with some twenty-seven! In the East Midlands, Leicester's two garages had a combined total of twenty-nine Fleetlines and nearby Wigston Garage received another eight. Additionally Stafford, Rugby and Nuneaton all had small numbers of these buses when they were new.

The allocation of small numbers of the DD12s when new was to twenty-one garages but, of the 199 buses, sixty-five were placed in service when new at garages in the West Midland Conurbation and a further fifty-six of them were operating on the intensive bus services in and around Leicester.

6023 was rebuilt in May 1968, when it was converted to a dual-door layout, though this central door was inserted in the second lower saloon bay rather than in the more usual central third bay. The bus became H43/28D after rebuilding and was sent to Sheepcote Street Garage in Birmingham, where it was not popular with the crews and, once into the suburbs, the centre exit was rarely used! 6023 was immediately employed on the new bus routes into the Stage One development of the Chelmsley

Wood Estate in Bosworth Drive. This huge overspill estate was built just outside the Birmingham boundary in Solihull on green-belt land and had an intended population of about 50,000. As the Corporation was not allowed to cross the city boundary with its bus services, the bus contracts into Chelmsley Wood were awarded to Midland Red, making it both a highly popular and remunerative service for them; the new Fleetlines were extensively used on these new, prestigious services.

Sixty-five DD12s were transferred to WMPTE on 3 December 1973 and all were repainted in WM's livery, many having a thin blue line at upper saloon floor level, similar to the style used on Birmingham's early Fleetlines. 5993/6/9/6009/11 and 6017 received all-over advertisements in the 1972 and 1973 period, while 6044 and 6054 both received the commemorative livery to celebrate HM Queen Elizabeth II's Silver Jubilee in 1977. All the DD12s transferred to West Midlands were withdrawn between 1978 and 1981, with 6045 soldiering on until that June.

Of the indigenous DD12s, 5995 was the first to go in May 1977, having suffered accident damage. 1978 saw twenty-six going, of which nineteen went to Paul Sykes for scrap. Withdrawals continued apace until the division of Midland Red into the North, East, South and West companies in September 1981. Of the survivors, twenty-nine went to Midland Red East, based at Southgate Street Garage, Leicester, with 6117 and 6135 surviving into early 1984. 6013/43/52 and 6095 went to Midland Red South, based in Leamington Spa. 6095 was converted to an open-topper, renumbered 990 and named *Lady Godiva*, lasting another four years in this guise. Midland Red West had just one of these Alexander-bodied Fleetlines, which was 6043, transferred from Midland Red South as a withdrawn bus but which was reinstated and somehow survived at Evesham Garage until December 1982. Another two passed to the Bristol Omnibus Co. to be converted to open top for use on the Weston-super-Mare 152 service from Sand Bay via the Promenade to Uphill. The buses were LHA 615F and LHA 623F, which became Bristol OC 8606 and 8605 respectively, both lasting until 1983. The surviving DD12 is 6015 (GHA 415G), which was restored by BaMMOT at the Wythall Bus Museum.

The final order for Daimler Fleetlines, although sourced from the same chassis and coach builder, were modified versions of the previous vehicles. Designated DD13, this order for 103 new buses was delivered in two batches, with seventy being delivered between June and November 1969 as 6156–6225 (SHA 856G–890G, UHA 191H–225H), with chassis numbers 63144–63213. A final thirty-three were received between November 1970 and January 1971, with fleet numbers 6261–6293 (YHA 261J–293J), which had chassis numbers 64280–64312. These buses had the upgraded Gardner 6LXB engine of 10.45 litres, while the Alexander bodywork was to their new J type style, having a different front panel below the windscreen. Following on from the trials with the dual-door converted 6023, these last Fleetlines were built with front entrance and centre exit doorways, a relocated staircase and an H45/30D seating layout. The DD13s, intended for OMO, had a two-step entrance and a higher flat-floor in the lower saloon, while the rear destination box was omitted, resulting in an even more plain rear profile.

As with previous vehicle allocations, these final two batches of Fleetlines were scattered across the system, although Digbeth Garage had the largest number with fifteen buses. Another thirty-one went to the seven Black Country garages and another eight were sent new to Redditch Garage. Only ten DD13s went to the two Leicester garages and another six were allocated to Nuneaton. Twelve garages had penny numbers of the DD13s, with Banbury Garage getting their only brand-new Daimler Fleetline. The last of the first batch, 6225 (UHA 225H), entered service in November 1969. This bus was the only DD13 to be preserved.

Fifty DD13s were transferred to WMPTE on 3 December 1973, of which twenty-six came from the first seventy while twenty-four were from the final thirty-three YHA---J registered buses. All were painted in WMPTE livery and 6186–7/98–6200/202/4/10–13/23 from the earlier batch and 6268/80–1/87–89 retained their original double-door layout. The two-door layout had become increasingly unpopular, as there had been several fatal accidents when passengers were trapped in the central door. This problem was partially solved when buses were fitted with a gearbox/door interlink, preventing the bus from moving before the central door was closed. This reduced accidents but considerably slowed the loading time, resulting in the PTE converting the DD13s to a single-door layout with the centre exit removed. Although this task was never completed, thirty-two of the PTE buses were rebuilt to a H45/31F layout between November 1975 and January 1978. All the DD13s retained by Midland Red kept their two-door layout. The first of the DD13s acquired by WMPTE to be withdrawn was 6269 in 1978. During the next three years, forty-four buses had been withdrawn. This left 6166, 6224/68/86/89 and 6290 lasting until 1982.

The earliest bus to be modified was 6198, which, in December 1970, was re-equipped with a SCG fully automatic gearbox. 6181 and 6209 were fitted with CAV fully automatic gearboxes in July 1975, as was 6183 during September 1975. Withdrawals began in October 1980, when 6163/80 were both taken out of service after being involved in accidents. 6177 went for the same reason in August 1981. In September 1981, when the Midland Red company was split into four component parts, Midland Red North received twelve DD13s. Midland Red East had twenty-one from the first batch and just two, 6284 and 6285, from the YHA---J batch. The Midland Red East fleet had all gone by 1986, save for 6222, which survived at Southgate Street until February 1990. Of the Midland Red North buses, seven remained in service until October 1986 and all were sold to Ribble Motor Services as their 1726–1733 lasting for up to another three years. Meanwhile Midland Red South had eight DD13s from the first batch and six from the second batch. The Midland Red DD13s retained by the new South company generally lasted longer, but the most unusual survivor was 6182. This Fleetline was converted to an open-topper, had the centre exit removed and was reseated to an O45/32F layout. Given the name *Warwick Castle* and renumbered 991, it ran in this condition from June 1985 until it was withdrawn and sold to the Guide Friday Company of Stratford-upon-Avon, who used it for another two years.

The 303 Alexander-bodied Daimler Fleetlines were bought at a time when Midland Red had failed to develop their own OMO bus, which was the way forward. By 1963, the advanced BMMO D9 was 'last year's model' and the D10 project had too many design problems to make it a practical and economic possibility. The Fleetlines were a good buy and, for many years, were the backbone of the company's double-deck operation, with some even surviving after the break-up of Midland Red in September 1981.

5257, 5257HA

5257, (5257HA), an almost new Daimler Fleetline CRG6LX with an Alexander H44/33F body, is at the bus stands in Exchange Street in front of Brinton's Carpet building in the centre of Kidderminster. The bus has yet to have its illuminated advertisement panel uncovered. It is working on the 132 service from Birmingham to Bewdley. 5257 was new to Digbeth Garage in May 1963 and would see further service with City of Oxford MS after its withdrawal in October 1976. (P. Tizard)

5259, 5259 HA

5259, (5259 HA), was one of the fifty of the DD11 class Daimler Fleetline CRG6LXs with Alexander A type bodies to enter service with Midland Red in April 1963. It was converted to one man operation in December 1969 and was one of the twenty-one of the type to pass to WMPTE on 3 December 1973. These were the only Daimler Fleetlines to have opening ventilators in the front upper saloon windows, which gave them almost a surprised-eyebrow look! 5259 in WMPTE livery has just turned out of Edgbaston Street after leaving the Bull Ring Bus Station and is turning right into Dudley Street when working on the 113 service to the Hardwick Arms via Perry Barr and College Road. (D. R. Harvey collection)

5282, 5282 HA

5282, (5282 HA), turns into Abbey Street after leaving St Margaret's Bus Station on the L29 route to Scraptoft, which was a Leicester local service. The bus was allocated from new to Leicester's Southgate Street Garage in March 1963, and is sufficiently new that its illuminated nearside advertisement panel has yet to be brought into use. With their large V-shaped windscreens these buses looked really modern when they first entered service and their success inevitably spelled the end for D9 production after 1966. Following the Midland Red is Leicester Corporation 212, (SJF 212), a Weymann-bodied Leyland Tiger Cub dating from 1958. (R. H. G. Simpson)

5998, GHA 398D

Awaiting more passengers in Pool Meadow Bus Station, Coventry, on 29 May 1967 is 5998, (GHA 398D). It is being used on the 590 service to Stratford-upon-Avon by way of Kenilworth, and is already filling up with passengers who have to wait for the crew to complete their tea break. This was one of the first DD12s; this Daimler Fleetline CRG6LX with an Alexander H44/33F body was new only eight months earlier in September 1966, working from Leamington Garage. (G. Pattison)

6023, GHA 423D

Leaving Sheepcote Street Garage in Birmingham and about to take up its duty from Birmingham bus station is 6023, (GHA 423D). This Alexander-bodied Daimler Fleetline CRG6LX was delivered as a standard seventy-seven-seater in December 1966 but was rebuilt to a H43/28D layout with a new central exit in May 1968. This bus then acted as a trial vehicle with OMO equipment before the DD13 dual-door buses were ordered, mainly on the services to the new Chelmsley Wood Estate. It passed to WMPTE on 3 December 1973 and was withdrawn in October 1978. (L. Mason)

6032, GHA 432D

In early NBC days, without the broad white stripe, one of Leamington Garage's DD12s is parked in Pool Meadow Bus Station in Coventry. 6032, (GHA 432D), is about to leave on a journey to Stratford on the 518 service. It had entered service in December 1966 and had been transferred to Leamington Garage when exactly four years old. The DD12 chassis was the Mark II version of the Daimler Fleetline CRG6LX, which had an inspection hatch on the nearside of the rear engine bustle. (D. R. Harvey collection)

6044 JHA 44E
Parked in Gravel Street at the rear of St Margaret's Bus Station in Leicester is 6044 (JHA 44E), a
DD12 class Daimler Fleetline CRG6LX with an Alexander H44/33F body. It entered service in
April 1967 and in 1977 was one of the double-deckers chosen to receive the overall silver livery
to commemorate the Queen's Silver Jubilee. When the last of Leicester's D9s were withdrawn,
6044 was taken out of store and returned to service from Southgate Street in November 1979. In
NBC livery, the bus is working on the 165 route. (P. Redmond)

6067, JHA 67E
Birmingham's Bull Ring Bus Station was built under the Bull Ring Centre and, with an entrance
in Station Street and an exit into Edgbaston Street, was opened on 1 November 1963. Buses in
Birmingham traditionally had their termini in the city centre streets and, although it was a very
useful asset, the location of the bus station was some distance from the main shopping area.
Coupled with its almost subterranean nature, it became a fume-filled, rundown, unpopular place
and was closed on 20 June 1999. 6067, (JHA 67E), new in June 1967, is about to work on the X7
express service, when the bus station still looked loved. This route used Stand No. 10 and operated
over the existing 147 route as a limited stop service to Redditch. (D. R. Harvey collection)

6086, JHA 86E

Standing in St Margaret's Bus Station in 1968 are three Daimler Fleetline CRG6LXs with Alexander H44/33F bodies. The leading bus is 6086, (JHA 86E), which has just arrived in the bus station from Syston when working on the 617 route. 6086 had entered service in July 1967 from Sandacre Garage in Leicester before being moved to Swadlincote in February 1970. It is in its original livery but, as with all the DD11 and 12 buses, does not display any clue to it being built by Daimler, but it has a large traditional BMMO badge on the front panel. (R. Crane)

6109, LHA 609F

Travelling up Fryer Street from the distant Broad Street in Wolverhampton is 6109, (LHA 609F). It is working on the 885 route from Kidderminster via Hagley, Stourbridge and Wombourne on a journey taking 1 hour 15 minutes. The 885 route was considered to be a very busy and remunerative service for Midland Red. The driver of this OMO service is checking his running board as he turns into Railway Drive, where it will terminate in front of the former LMS Wolverhampton Low Level railway station. (D. R. Harvey collection)

6158, SHA 858G

Standing in Cannock Garage yard on 27 April 1985 in Chaserider livery is 6158, (SHA 858G). This was the third of the seventy DD13 Daimler Fleetline CRG6LXB with Alexander H44/30D bodies. They were built with a centre exit layout based on the prototype 6023. 6158 entered service in July 1969 at Stafford Garage and was eventually moved to Cannock, from where it passed to Midland Red (North) Ltd, where it was used until July 1986. The bus is in the purple striped Chaserider livery. (D. R. Harvey)

6195, UHA 195H

Travelling through Thurmaston when working on the 615 service is 6195, (UHA 195H). On 8 February 1979, the bus, a Daimler Fleetline CRG6LXB with an Alexander H44/30D body is painted in the uninspired NBC livery of all-over poppy red with a white mid-deck band. The bus had entered service in September 1969 and survived until the same month in 1981. Even at this date, the line of cars behind the bus is all British-built with such delights as a Ford Escort, a Morris Marina, a Mini Clubman saloon and a Triumph 2000 saloon. (D. R. Harvey)

6204, UHA 204H

6204, (UHA 204H), stands at Carlyle Road Works on 14 September 1969 when newly delivered from the Alexander factory in Falkirk and is displaying its Midland Red D13 class type in the destination number box. These Daimler Fleetline CRG6LXB had the Alexander J type bodywork, which had two-step entrance and exits, and a flat floor along the length of the lower saloon. 6204 went into service at Harts Hill Garage in Brierley Hill and was transferred to West Midlands PTE on 3 December 1973. (R. F. Mack)

6210, UHA 210J

Travelling into Old Square from Priory Queensway with the 1960 Maple House behind it is 6210, (UHA 210J), working in the 171 service from Water Orton. This was after it was taken over by West Midlands PTE on 3 December 1973. 6210 was repainted in West Midlands livery and was withdrawn in 1981, which was about normal for the Daimler Fleetlines transferred to WMPTE; this was about three years before the Midland Red companies began to take them out of service. (A. J. Douglas)

6285, UHA 285J

Above: Travelling along Melton Road in Syston is 6285, (UHA 285J), wearing the final NBC poppy red and white band livery. It is working on the 617 route service on 9 February 1979. This was one of the final thirty-three Daimler Fleetlines CRG6LXBs with Alexander H45/30D J type bodywork entering service in January 1971. The bus went to the Leicester area at the end of 1978 and was at this time operating from Sandacre Garage. The bus passed to Midland Red East on 6 September 1981 and lasted another four years before it was withdrawn. (D. R. Harvey collection)

6272, YHA 272J

Opposite above: The last thirty-three Fleetlines had the more powerful Gardner 6LXB 10.45-litre engine, which at 1,850 rpm produced 180 hp. The seating capacity of all the dual-door DD13s had been reduced by two to an H45/30D layout, while these last buses had a different frontal design below the windscreen in the style of a gaping mouth! 6272, (YHA 272J), new in December 1970, stands in Bidford-on-Avon on 22 September 1981, a matter of days after becoming part of the Midland Red South bus fleet. (F. W. York)

6280, YHA 280J

Opposite below: After the Midland Red services in Birmingham and the Black Country were taken over by West Midlands PTE on 3 December 1973, as a temporary measure all of the 413 former Midland Red buses that were roadworthy had red-backed fablon stickers to cover up the Midland Red fleetnames. This was still in the near future, however, for Alexander-bodied Daimler Fleetline CRG6LXB 6280, (YHA 280), as it travels into Navigation Street when working on the 114 route to Sutton Coldfield via Falcon Lodge in 1972 with the final style of Midland Red fleet name. It is passing the site of the now long-demolished Queens Hotel and the terminus for buses going to Kidderminster and Stourport, and is being followed by the Birmingham Guy Arab IV Sp 3059, (MOF 59), that was bought for, but failed to be, preserved. (L. Mason)

Stratford Blue Taken Over

The takeover of Midland Red by the National Bus Company was caused by the BET Group deciding to sell its interests in road transport. This happened in March 1969 and, with that takeover, the attractive and individualistic mid-blue-and-white livery disappeared from Stratford and was replaced by the corporate blandness of NBC red. Smaller operators had to go, as they did not fit with the new image, and Stratford-upon-Avon Blue Motors was finally absorbed by the parent Midland Red on January 1971, just as the final Alexander-bodied Daimler Fleetlines were being delivered to the parent company. They took over forty-nine buses and repainted them in the comparatively drab Midland Red livery, adding 2000 to the Stratford Blue fleet numbers. The garages at Stratford and Kineton were kept open. All of the Leyland Titan PD3 front-engine double-deckers were sold to the Isle of Man Road Services in 1972, while the three Atlanteans went to City of Oxford.

(1–6), 2001–2006 668–673 HNX

These six Leyland Titan PD3A/1s had Willowbrook bodies with an H41/32F layout. They had synchromesh gearboxes, air brakes and the recently developed glass-fibre St Helen's full-width bonnet assembly. 1–6 were delivered in December 1963 and January 1964 to replace Leyland-bodied Titan PD2/1s of 1948 and 1950, and were used mainly on the Birmingham and Oxford services. They were sold to Isle of Man Road Services in 1972, being re-registered MN 44–45 and 63–66.

(7–8), 2007–2008 GUE 1–2D

This pair of Willowbrook-bodied Leyland Titan PD3A/1s were virtually the same as 1–6, being fitted with a St Helen's full-width bonnet, a synchromesh gearbox and air brakes. Delivered in January 1966, they were withdrawn by Midland Red in the summer of 1972 and sold to Isle of Man Road Services with Manx registrations MN 2670–2671.

(9–11), 2009–2011 NAC 415–417F

Delivered in December 1967, three rear-engined Leyland Atlantean PDR1A/1s with NCME H44/31F bodywork arrived. They were sold just five months after the Midland

Red takeover and went to City of Oxford Motor Services as their 904–906. The former 10 is now preserved by the Oxford Bus Museum.

(20), 2020 TNX 454

This was the sole survivor of three Leyland Titan PD2/12s fitted with Willowbrook H35/28RD bodies and delivered in March 1956. It was only in Midland stock for four months.

(36–39), 2024–2027 536–539 EUE

For the four January 1963 deliveries of exposed radiator Leyland Titan PD3/4s, the body order went to Northern Counties with the same H41/32F seating plan. As with all the Stratford Blue fleet, these buses were taken over on 1 January 1971 and were sold to Isle of Man Road Services at the end of that year, being re-registered MN 57–60.

(17–19), 2028–2030 2767–2769 NX

These three Leyland Titan PD3/4 were the first 30-foot-long double-deckers in the fleet and had Willowbrook H41/32F bodies. The PD3/4 had a synchromesh gearbox, air brakes and exposed radiators, and were delivered in February and March 1960. They were sold to Isle of Man Road Services and re-registered MN 41–43.

Last Orders

The last double-deckers ordered by Midland Red were thirty Leyland Atlantean PDR1A/1s with Metro-Cammell H43/29D bodies. The buses were completed but were never delivered to Midland Red and were diverted to London Country as their AN91–120 and were registered MPJ 1901L–220L. They all entered service in October and November 1972.

2020, TNX 454

The only one of the three Leyland Titan PD2/12s with attractive Willowbrook H35/28RD bodies to survive into Midland Red ownership was TNX 454, numbered 20 in the Stratford Blue fleet. It is parked in the Bridgefoot bus station alongside the Red Lion Public House. It had been delivered in March 1956 but was never given its allotted Midland Red number and was sold to G&G Coaches of Leamington and gave another three years' service. (P. Yeomans)

2019, 2769 NX

Turning out of Moor Street in Birmingham at the height of the rebuilding of the Bull Ring is Stratford Blue 19, (2769 NX), working on the 150 service to Stratford-upon-Avon via Henley-in-Arden in 1962. In the background is the huge Market Hall, designed by Charles Edge and opened on 12 February 1835 with 600 market stalls. The building was faced with stone from Bath and its wide entrances were supported by Doric columns. It is already closed prior to demolition. The bus was one of three Leyland Titan PD3/4 with Willowbrook H41/32F bodywork and was transferred to Midland Red on 1 January 1971. It was sold to the Isle of Man Road Services as their 41, (MN 41), in November of that year. (L. Mason)

2037, 537 EUE
Parked in Gloucester Green Bus Station in Oxford is 37, (537 EUE), a Northern Counties-bodied Leyland Titan PD3/4 dating from January 1963. Later numbered 25 in the Stratford Blue fleet, it is operating on the 44 service to Stratford via Woodstock, Chipping Norton and Shipston-on-Stour. This journey took 2 hours and 23 minutes through the delightful north Oxfordshire and south Warwickshire countryside. The bus has an illuminated offside advertisement panel, which is promoting Flowers Keg Bitter, brewed in Stratford. (D. R. Harvey collection)

2001, 668 HNX
Standing in Station Approach in front of the former LNWR's Leamington Avenue Station is 1, (668 HNX), the first of the St Helens concealed front buses purchased by Stratford Blue in December 1963. This Leyland Titan PD3A/1 had a Willowbrook H41/32F body. This was the standard layout for all Stratford Blue's PD3s. The bus is about to work on the 32A service to Kineton via Gaydon. Behind the bus, in the station, is a British Railways English Electric Type 4 Diesel Electric 1Co-Co1 locomotive. (D. R. Harvey collection)

2005, 672 HNX

Once taken over from Stratford Blue, most of the fleet was quickly repainted in Midland Red's unrelieved all-over red livery and, as a result, looked considerably duller. 2005, (672 HNX), formerly fleet number 5 with Stratford Blue, is a Willowbrook H41/32F-bodied Leyland Titan PD3A/1, fitted with the new one-piece destination box. It is travelling along Stratford Road in Shirley and is passing the mock-Elizabethan Saracen's Head Public House. It is working on the 150 service to Stratford-upon-Avon and would soon be sold to the Isle of Man Road Services as their 66, (MN 66). (L. Mason)

2007, GUE 1D

The first of the last pair of Leyland Titan PD3A/1 with Willowbrook H41/32F bodywork was 7, (GUE 1D). This was delivered in January 1966 and again had the St Helens-type concealed radiator and bonnet assembly. It is passing along Oxford Street in the historic village of Woodstock, close to Blenheim Palace, while employed on the 44 service to Oxford. This was jointly operated with the City of Oxford Motor Services and Long Compton was where the buses used to cross and the passengers had to re-book. Here crews changed buses and the parcels service often swapped packages if there was a short working or extra being operated by either operator. (R. H. G. Simpson)

2008, GUE 2D

Having left the Bull Ring Bus Station at its Edgbaston Street exit, Stratford Blue 8, (GUE 2D), is working on the 150 service, which was jointly operated with Midland Red and took 72 minutes to travel the 23 miles between Birmingham and Stratford-upon-Avon. This was the last front-engined, half-cab double-decker to be bought by Stratford Blue. Behind the Leyland Titan PD3A/1 is Midland Red 4858, (858 KHA), a very early Carlyle-bodied BMMO D9, working on the 111 route to Roughley. (D. Williams)

2009, (NAC 415F)

The last buses delivered new to Stratford Blue were three Leyland Atlantean PDR1A/1 with rather ugly Northern Counties H44/31F bodywork. 9, (NAC 415F), is parked at the Bridgefoot Bus Station in 1968. After six years of purchasing Leyland Titan PD3s, in 1967 Stratford Blue management took the plunge and bought three rear-engined double-deckers that were delivered that December. Their masters at Bearwood were already purchasing 'proprietary brands' of buses, in this case the Daimler Fleetline. Stratford Blue, perversely, as if wanting to show their independence from Midland Red management, went their own way and bought the highbridge version of the Leyland Atlantean, the PDR1A/1s, which had the 0.680 11.1-litre Leyland engine. (D. Williams)

The Harper Brothers Connection

Harper Brothers had been founded in the 1920s, centred on the mining village of Heath Hayes and operating extensive services to Cannock, Lichfield, Aldridge, Brownhills, Hednesford, Kingstanding and eventually gaining access to Carrs Lane in Birmingham. After Midland Red had compulsorily lost its West Midland's heartland operations to WMPTE, the newly formed Midland Red Omnibus Co. became somewhat predatory and the business of Harper Brothers of Heath Hayes, a doyen of independent bus operators in the West Midlands, was taken over on 7 September 1974 in order to strengthen its operations to the north of Birmingham. The buses had 2200 added to their original Harpers Brothers fleet numbers. At the twilight of the front-engined double-deck era they had standardised on Leyland Titan PD3A/1s, but between 1970 and 1973 purchased three pairs of Daimler Fleetlines and ordered another two, which were delivered, after some delay, to Midland Red Omnibuses.

After the takeover these six Fleetlines and the Leyland PD3s all remained at the Heath Hayes Garage until it was closed, when they were transferred to Cannock in February 1977, eventually being absorbed into the Midland Red North fleet in September 1981.

(1, 3, 6–7), 2201 JXN 349, 2203 OLD 280, 2206 KXW 284, 2207 KYY 770

These were the remnants of a fleet of Leyland Titan 7RTs, with the first two having Park Royal H30/26R bodies built in 1948 and 1954, and the other two, both built in 1950, having Weymann and MCCW bodies. They were ex-London Transports RTL 26, 1600, 500 and 800.

(8–9), 2208 BDJ 802, 2209 BDJ 807

This pair of AEC Regent III 0961RT types with London Transport-style Park Royal H30/26R were built for St Helen's as their D2 and D7. Both were withdrawn immediately after the takeover in September 1974.

(11), 2211 888 DUK

This was a former Strachan demonstrator built in 1963. It was a Guy Arab V 6LW Strachan H41/31F and was not operated by Midland Red.

(23), 2223 NRF 349F

This was the last half-cab double-decker to be purchased. Arriving in May 1965 this Leyland PD3A/5 had a pneumocyclic gearbox, air brakes and St Helen's-style concealed radiator. The bodywork was by NCME with a H40/32RD layout and was withdrawn in January 1977.

(25), 2225 SBF 233

This was the last 7-foot 6-inch-wide double-decker purchased, arriving in January 1962. The chassis was the quite rare Leyland PD2/28, equipped with an enclosed radiator, a manual gearbox and air brakes. At some point the Midland Red-style concealed radiator had a St Helen's front grill grafted onto it. The bus had a NCME H36/28RD body. It became a driver trainer in February 1976, before its conversion into a tow lorry. It then passed to Midland Red North and is now preserved.

(24, 26), 2224, 2226 LRF 992–993F

These two Leyland PD3A/1 were both delivered in March 1965. They had synchromesh gearboxes, air brakes and the recently developed glass-fibre St Helen's concealed radiator and bonnet assembly. The bodywork was built by NCME. They had short lives with Midland Red after the takeover, being withdrawn in January 1977.

(27–28), 2227–2228 HBF 679–680D

This pair of 8-foot-wide Leyland PD2A/27s were delivered in January 1966 with MCW Orion H36/28RD bodywork. They had St Helen's enclosed radiators, synchromesh gearbox and air brakes. Withdrawn in 1976 and 1977, both eventually became driver training vehicles.

(29–30), 2229–2230 JBF 405–406H

These were the first pair of Daimler Fleetline CRG6LXs, delivered as 29 and 30 in the Harpers fleet in May 1970. They had NCME H44/33F bodies. After the takeover in September 1981 they saw further service with Midland Red North.

(31–32), 2231–2232 BRE 311–312J

The second pair of Daimler Fleetline CRG6LXs also had Northern Counties H44/33F bodywork, being delivered in July 1971 as Harpers 31 and 32. They also saw further service with Midland Red North.

(33–34), 2233–2234 TRE948–949L

The final pair of Daimler Fleetline CRG6LXs arrived in April 1973 as 33 and 34. The bodywork this time was built by ECW, also with a H44/33F layout.

439–440 (JOX 439P–440P)

Two more ECW H44/33F-bodied Daimler Fleetlines CRG6LXs were ordered by Harper Brothers before the September 1974 takeover, but their delivery was delayed until March 1976, whereupon they were delivered to Midland Red, numbered 439–440 and classified D14s.

Green Bus, Rugeley

This long-established company was founded in 1927 by C. J. Whieldon and had services in the Uttoxeter, Cannock and Lichfield operating area. Green Bus was taken over by Midland Red on 5 November 1973. The buses were all given fleet numbers, but were sold in February 1974.

2171–4 VFM 596/620/624/RFM 435

Bristol Lodekka LD6B ECW H33/25RD, b. 1955 ex-Crosville DLB 731/755/759/690.

2175–6 504/501 BRB

Bristol Lodekka FSF6B ECW H34/26f, b. 1960 ex-Cumberland 503/500.

2177 LJX 18

AEC Regent V MCCW H40/32F, b. 1960 ex-Hebble 18.

Acquired Buses

967 XVT
Daimler Fleetline CRG6LX NCME H40/33F 1963, ex-PMT 967 7/1975 for spares.

970 XVT
Daimler Fleetline CRG6LX NCME H40/33F 1963, ex-PMT 970 7/1975 for spares.

2972 972 XVT
Daimler Fleetline CRG6LX NCME H40/33F 1963, ex-PMT 972 12/1978 for spares.

2974 974 XVT
Daimler Fleetline CRG6LX NCME H40/33F 1963, ex-PMT 974 12/1978 for spares.

2790 790 EVT
Leyland Atlantean PDR1/1 Weymann L39/34F, b. 1962 ex-PMT 790 12/1978 for spares.

2825 825 KVT
Leyland Atlantean PDR1/1 Weymann L39/34F, b. 1962 ex-PMT 825 12/1978.

2905 905 UVT
Leyland Atlantean PDR1/1 Weymann L39/34F, b. 1962, ex-PMT 905 12/1978 for spares.

2907 907 UVT
Leyland Atlantean PDR1/1 Weymann L39/34F, b. 1962 ex-PMT 907 12/1978 for spares.

2910 910 UVT
Leyland Atlantean PDR1/1 Weymann L39/34F, b. 1962 ex-PMT 910 12/1978.

2223, NRF 349F
Leyland Titan PD3A/5 2223, (NRF 349F), had a Northern Counties H40/32RD body and had entered service with Harper Brothers in May 1968 as their 23. Like all the rest of the Harper fleet it was acquired on 7 September 1974, but it was the only one of the three PD3s to have a pneumocyclic gearbox. It did have, in common with the other two buses, a St Helens-style full-width bonnet and air brakes. The rear entrance NCME bodywork seemed to have a very long overhang. It is working towards Cannock on the 854 service and has been repainted in NBC red. (D. R. Harvey collection)

2225, SBF 233

Harper Brothers 25, (SBF 233), was the only Leyland Titan PD2/28 built; it was 7 feet 6 inches wide, had airbrakes and, originally, a Midland Red-style concealed radiator, although this was altered in 1970 to having a St Helens radiator cowl tacked on to the existing bonnet. It had a H36/28RD four-bay construction body built by Northern Counties and entered service in January 1962. After withdrawal it was immediately converted to a Midland Red driver trainer in February 1976 before being converted to a towing lorry, in which state it was sold for preservation. (D. R. Harvey)

2226, LRF 993F

The second of the two Northern Counties-bodied Leyland Titan PD3A/1s, 26, (LRF 993F), stands in Cannock bus station and is about to return in service to its garage at Heath Hayes. It was built in March 1968 with a synchromesh gearbox, air brakes and St Helens-style full-width bonnet. Like its twin it was withdrawn in January 1977 and eventually turned up with Allander of Milngavie, but sadly it was never operated. (J. Walker)

2227, HBF 679D

The sight of the green-and-white winged buses of Harper Brothers in service in the centre of Birmingham was something of a shock as no independent operator had breached the Corporation's monopoly within the boundaries of the city. On 21 June 1965, Harper Brothers, who had operated from Lichfield to the Odeon at Kingstanding Circle for many years, began their Cannock service from Union Street. 27, (HBF 679D), a Leyland Titan PD2A/27 with a Metro-Cammell H36/28RD Orion body dating from January 1966, swings around Old Square (by now part of the Priory Ringway Inner Ring Road) in front of Lewis's Department Store as it travels on a short working to Heath Hayes. (R. F. Mack)

2232, BRE 312J

Parked in Cannock bus station is Harper Brothers 32, (BRE 312J). Bodied by Northern Counties, this Daimler Fleetline CRG6LX entered service from Heath Hayes in July 1971 and was only in the green-and-white Harper's livery until soon after the takeover by Midland Red on 7 September 1974. Seating seventy-five passengers, the slightly lower height of these buses made them look longer than they actually were. (A. J. Douglas)

2234, TRE 949L

On an awful day in January 1984, 2234, (TRE 949L), a Daimler Fleetline CRG6LX that had formerly been Harpers 34, (TRE 949L), travels into Navigation Street when working on the 158 route in the Chaserider livery of Midland Red North. Behind the bus and opposite the Austin FX4 taxi in Stephenson Street is Hudson's Bookshop, famous for its large shelf space for road and rail transport. This was the last double-decker delivered new to Harper Brothers, arriving in April 1973, by which time the company had switched coach builder allegiance to Eastern Counties. (D. R. Harvey)

439 JOX 439P

Ordered by Harper Brothers, JOX 439P, the first of a pair of Daimler Fleetline CRG6LXs with Eastern Counties H43/33F bodywork, stands in Heath Hayes yard in Midland Red livery. This was numbered 439 by Midland Red and it and its twin, 440, were the last double-deck buses to enter service with Midland Red, with this occurring in March 1976. This was quite a late example of the ECW body to have the flat two-piece windscreen. After 440, (JOX 440P), a number of second-hand buses, nearly all Alexander-bodied Daimler Fleetlines were acquired mainly from Potteries Motor Traction, but nearly all were bought for their spare parts and were not operated. (D. R. Harvey collection)